I read this absorbing book in one sitting, and couldn't stop until finishing. Relating to many of the deeply personal stories at a visceral level, I recognized similar stories in myself. After reading, it took hours of mental and emotional processing to fully appreciate the beauty and elegance of this impactful volume. It uniquely combines philosophy, psychology and spirituality with practical exercises to illuminate the pathway to an examined life. "New Stories of Love, Power, and Purpose" makes the pursuit of human depth both approachable and worthwhile.

Doug Kirkpatrick, Author of The No-Limits Enterprise, Forbes Speaker, Organizational Advisor.
USA

We are at a time of deep transformation in human history and Christiane's book shines a light for a path forward into the Unknown. It is a very unique mix of knowledge, personal story and practices and is what I sense we are being called towards as the human species at this time in our evolutionary history: illuminated and energized by the alchemical combination of love, power and purpose and with practical ways to find our unique form of resonance with that field.

Nikki Thompson, Life Coach and Land Custodian,
Australia

Christiane's personal journey, bravely shared, anchors New Stories of Love, Power, and Purpose. Passionately told, intimate, and refreshingly concrete, Christiane expertly weaves a story of stories revealing the interplay between deeply personal and diverse topics. Both compelling and practical, Christiane gives the reader actionable tools and practices to help reveal and refine one's own relationship with love, power, purpose, and work. I found the book, as the author claims, an excellent "guide for all who seek greater alignment between what we care about, how we influence the world, and how we organize with others." Highly recommend it!

**Thomas Thomison, Co-founder HolacracyOne, LLC,
Founding Member encode.org llc
USA**

This book had me gripped from the first page. It comes at a time when the world and humanity really need to get access to the universal and inherent power of love, to stop the power abuse, war and violence to each other and all living creatures on this beautiful earth, and get a clear sense of purpose and direction, to break free from the victim-perpetrator cycle. This book is so easy to read – the first part mostly expressed through personal stories that touch the heart and move deeply, while opening one profound insight after the other. The second part is a step-by-step guidance through the wonderful JournaLogue practice. I was already familiar with that practice since I participated in one of Christiane's workshops last year, but I am delighted to be able to recommend this book to all my friends and colleagues who are also on a path of conscious evolution, individually and collectively.

At the end of the book there is an invitation to a global community that applies these principles and methods. I really look forward to being part of that.

**Hanna Hühndorf, Landscape Gardener and Meditation Coach
Germany**

Christiane opens up to her readers in a unique way and from the depth of her personal story she offers everything that emerged from and through her. I could feel so much resonance throughout the book, which showed me repeatedly that what I read is relevant and needed now. What you find is a fascinating mixture of personal depth, of pointing towards those who supported and nourished her journey, and finally the practical application and the invitation to go on your own individual and collective journey.

Anke Lessmann, Co-founder Bewusstes Unternehmen, Germany

NEW STORIES OF LOVE, POWER, AND PURPOSE

A GLOBAL INVITATION TO EXPERIMENT WITH THE UNKNOWN

CHRISTIANE SEUHS-SCHOELLER

Copyright © 2022 Christiane Seuhs-Schoeller.

All Rights Reserved. This book contains material protected under International and Federal Copyright Laws and Treaties. Any unauthorized reprint or use of this material is prohibited. No part of this book may be reproduced or transmitted in any form or by any means, electronic or mechanical, including photocopying, recording, or by any information storage and retrieval system without express written permission from the author/publisher.

ISBN: 978-1-64184-794-0 (Hardcover)
ISBN: 978-1-64184-792-6 (Paperback)
ISBN: 978-1-64184-793-3 (Ebook)

To my son Conrad.

TABLE OF CONTENTS

Foreword xiii
Introduction xvii

Chapter 1: The Ordeal of Shifting into the "New World of Work" 1
    Against the wall 5
    Endings and new beginnings 7
    Why change the way we organize? 8
    Explorations of power. 11
    Pathways for organizing 14
    Explorations of the New World of Work 15
    What's missing? 16
    Deep unlearning and new learning 20

Chapter 2: Everything is Connected 23
    The human cost of the race for success 26
    The blossoming of a movement 29
    Voices of intuition 31
    The evolutionary principle of the universe 32

Chapter 3: Understanding What is Holding Us Back 34
    Fear 40
    Overwhelm 41
    Facing fear and overwhelm 45
    Hearing the call 48

Chapter 4: Four Shared Stories of the Global Community . . 50
    The story of stories. 50
    The story of purpose. 54
    The story of power 81
    The story of love 100

Chapter 5: A Story of Love, Power, and Purpose 122
    A life in balance 124
    Emerging experiments 128
    The burden of not knowing 132
    The relief of not knowing. 134
    The invitation. 135

Chapter 6: The JournaLogue 137
    Journaling as a spiritual practice 141
    Two ways to proceed. 143

Phase 1: Outer and Inner Conditions 144
    Exercise I: getting started 144
    Exercise II: your Sacred Space 149
    Exercise III: your personal SCENARIO. 153

Phase 2: Your Inner Support Team 158
    Exercise IV: connecting to SOURCE. 158
    Exercise V: welcoming LOVE 164
    Exercise VI: love your POWER 168
    Exercise VII: the welcome ritual. 172
    Exercise VIII: yay for the small things! 176

    Exercise IX: befriending your SABOTEUR 183
    Exercise X: support, support, support 196
    Exercise XI: Practice. Connection. Anytime.
        Anywhere. 200
Phase 3: Activating Your Resources. 204
    Exercise XII: knowing why. 204
    Exercise XIII: your wisdom 206
    Exercise XIV: your core psychological needs. 211
    Exercise XV: favorable conditions. 217
Phase 4: Your SCENARIO 220
    An ongoing experiment with the unknown. 220

Chapter 7: Your Gifts Meet the World's Needs. 221
    Calling out to you. 223
    From now forward 225

Acknowledgements. 227
About the Author 231

Foreword

The Secret Sauce: Not Knowing is Most Intimate

There is a Zen Koan I love. It is only six lines long, with the punchline being: "Not Knowing is Most Intimate." The first time I read those words, I felt something inside me click. Somehow, somewhere, this internal voice said, "Of course!" Simultaneously, I laughed a big belly Buddha laugh, and my body relaxed. Zen sure has a knack for getting to the essence of a thing. And Christiane Seuhs-Schoeller has a talent for unpacking essence into full-throated stories chock full of wisdom.

In her book, New Stories of *Love, Power, and Purpose; A Global Invitation to Experiment With the Unknown*, Christiane makes a case for standing confidently in uncertainty. The unknown transforms from something feared to a gateway of abundance – a path to more love, power, and purpose in your life and your work. Like the Koan, Christiane claims "not knowing" is a most intimate condition signaling that you are indeed on the right path. In the author's own words, "There it was: the vastness, the liberation, the curiosity, the joy, the ease, the love, and the power of not knowing!" Sounds counterintuitive, huh? How could this possibly be true? How is "not knowing" the key to greater love, power, and purpose? Read on, dear reader, read on.

Her stories are poignant, instructive, and comforting. Christiane invites us to accompany her on a personal journey of discovery. We tag along as she dives deep into some of the most fundamental yet tricky aspects of being human. She reveals, for example, how surrender becomes a positive act, not a passive condition. Further, she argues that surrender is not simply giving up or being satisfied with whatever comes your way. But it has the same power as its close cousin uncertainty - both can transform. Again, in her own words, surrender becomes the act of "bringing your whole self to be of service, individually and collectively. To be of service to your own purpose, to a larger purpose, and ultimately to the greater whole." This two-step dance with "the unknown" and "surrender" forms a backdrop upon which she probes the depths of love, power, and purpose.

As Christiane suggests we all do, I have been running experiments on various aspects of my life: How I work, how I live day-to-day, and even how I love. Seeing life itself as a grand experiment has dramatically changed how I view myself and my work in the world. For example, motivated by frustration and cynicism, about 20 years ago, I began to experiment with radically new ways of working. Fed up with status quo options, I became ready and broken enough to re-evaluate my beliefs about how work gets done. It was terrifying at the time, and it meant I had to unlearn most of what I thought I knew and surrender to something greater than myself, something that was just beyond my grasp of understanding. But as I stepped into and confronted my fear, a world of opportunity opened.

Ultimately one thing led to another all those years ago as I danced with fear and uncertainty; eventually, in 2007, I found

New Stories of Love, Power, and Purpose

myself co-founder of HolacracyOne. Little did I know then, but this company would publish a set of rules, call the practice of those rules Holacracy™ and ultimately turn how work gets managed on its head. Fifteen years later, I am a different person with a changed view of what "an organization" is, a much deeper sense of my power, a sharper understanding of my purpose, and an abundance of love in all aspects of my life - even love of work! And dear reader, it was in the context of Holacracy practice where I first met Christiane some ten years ago.

I put to you that when Christiane invites us to experiment with the unknown, she invites us to develop a set of practices to lean on. Why? Because it is nearly impossible to apply principles alone. This book gives you concrete insights and tools to bridge the gap between theory and practice. As Christiane shares, "My deep experience of the connectedness of everything couldn't connect to "the world out there," and I came to a new question: what is the connection between my inner world and the outer expression of my work in the world?" Learning how to bridge between your interior passions and their concrete expressions is an essential theme of this book.

Christiane has been a friend and colleague for over a decade. I love her and her work. Our professional relationship is atypical - deeper, more authentic, and more intimate by virtue of the very experiments she is now suggesting you undertake. I invite you to get to know Christiane as I know her through the stories and practices she shares here. I promise you will be better in the doing.

Onward!

Thomas Thomison
Houston, Texas USA
May 2022

Introduction
Within, Without, With All... Approaches to Love, Power, and Purpose

Welcome, dear reader! It's my pleasure to invite you on a new exploration of self, other, and all. First, we'll explore the global movement toward greater alignment of love and power in service to purpose. Then, we'll look at a proven approach for cultivating greater expression of powerful love and loving power in our own lives and communities, and at the ripple effect of positive change that is triggered by such an approach.

In Chapters 1 through 5, we'll explore why there's such a profound hunger, worldwide, for the liberation of human wholeness in service to collective and planetary wellbeing. Through case studies and examples from my own life and the lives of clients and colleagues, we'll explore common pain points for those striving toward new ways of collaborating and then what becomes possible when these pain points are addressed.

In Chapter 6, we'll move into a step-by-step practice for deepening your connection to your own inner wisdom, love, and power. The JournaLogue is a practice that anyone can develop, and this step-by-step program will support you in learning this method for self-reflection, introspection, and self-discovery.

Finally, you'll be offered steps to apply these capacities to scenarios that hold great meaning for you, as an experiment in positively shifting almost any relationship or situation in your life. Acting in service to your purpose from a place of unified love and power, you'll be invited into a global community of those who recognize the potential of this movement toward soulful, purpose-aligned living and the possibility for ripple effects to shape collective outcomes.

As members of our planetary ecosystem and as co-creators of our human future, our lives are inextricably entwined. This book, therefore, simultaneously explores the personal *and* the collective. Join me on this path toward deepening integrity with self, other, and all.

1

The Ordeal of Shifting into the "New World of Work"

Since the beginning of the 21st century, there has been a rapidly growing global movement toward new forms of organizing—the "New World of Work"[1], as it is broadly called.

Contemporary social critiques often suggest that more wholeness, empathy, and communication are needed to humanize our workplaces, but few really address the underlying assumptions about power and influence upon which almost all modern human organizing is built. This book isn't focused on bringing more humanity to our corporate lives. Rather, it addresses larger issues that not only stand in the way of creating more humane working conditions, but impede, on the broadest scale, even those human endeavors that want to follow the call of serving people and planet

---

[1] What today is called the New World of Work has its roots in the works of Frithjof Bergman, a German/American professor of philosophy at the University of Michigan. He first coined the term "New Work" in the mid 1970s. https://en.wikipedia.org/wiki/Frithjof_Bergmann

equally. These issues are fundamentally related to power, and we'll explore new stories that can help to distribute power and responsibility where it really belongs—with each and every one of us.

As part of the field of organizing for three decades, I have experienced ups and downs, pains and gains, and the deep personal development journey that is often triggered by the search for more meaningful ways of working together. As I moved into a career in self-organization more than ten years ago, I began to see many people courageously stepping into this journey, and many being overwhelmed and harmed along the way. From my current vantage point, I can see that my work has created the conditions for both—nurturing wonderful experiences for some, and causing harm for others.

The management hierarchy, which anchors and legitimizes the expression of "power over" in organizational structures, is largely unquestioned by much of the business world. This form of power hierarchy often remains in play even in those fields where people attempt to explicitly institute new ways of working—standing as an invisible obstacle to the conscious exploration and embodiment of healthy power.

We cannot change systems while holding onto unconscious patterns that drive us. A true alternative can only work if we shift *the story of* and *our relationships with* power. These deep, foundational shifts must take place within systems *and* people. To use a common metaphor, we are fish swimming in the water of power dynamics—invisible, yet surrounding us on all sides. Once we are able to see our circumstances as they are—notice the water we are swimming in, so to speak—we can embark on journeys of discovery and experimentation. These journeys will support each of us, and all of us collectively, to develop new stories with unimaginable possibilities.

The management hierarchy as a requisite way of working—be it through businesses, nonprofit and non-governmental organizations, public or private institutions, social movements, or any other endeavor that gets people together to mutually reach a desired goal or outcome—has run its course. The power hierarchy has served us beautifully, but in the last century it has turned into a machine serving mainly itself. Combined with other societal developments, our default organizing system in contemporary society has become like a robot out of control, ultimately dominating our livelihood on all levels. Whatever our sector—health, education, politics, administration, sports, art, and more—we are confronted with the need to redefine our assumptions about how we work together.

Millions of people know and sense this, hence the many beautiful businesses, movements, conferences, offerings, and activities emerging around better ways for us humans to come together and engage collectively. Meaningful collective engagement serves both people and planet, and humanity is actively searching not only for ways to stop planetary destruction, but to secure our individual and collective livelihoods.

Dear reader, I hope that this work can serve as both a story of my own personal journey around love, power, and purpose *and* as a guide for all who seek greater alignment between what we care about, how we influence the world, and how we organize with others for our collective survival and flourishing. I'll share some discoveries that I believe are universal to the human experience, through the lens of my own biography. Then, together, we'll explore common patterns in the behavior of individuals and collectives going through the transformation from power hierarchies to evolutionary organizing. We'll explore some underlying causes for those patterns.

Here, you will find stories about the transformational journey involved in stepping out of hierarchical power dynamics—dynamics that have been at the core of our societies, globally, for millennia. You'll read about the common obstacles people and groups encounter on that journey, and what limits many of these endeavors' success. You'll learn from others' oscillations between hope and disappointment, and read stories about overcoming the obstacles that are holding us back.

As your guide on this exploration of love, power, and purpose, I want to introduce myself. I am an Austrian entrepreneur and a global citizen, a nomad, currently mainly based in Greece;

a mother and an aunt; a daughter and a sister, the youngest of six girls. I have been an employee, a CEO, and an entrepreneur for over three decades and an international organizational and leadership development coach and consultant for over two decades. At every step of my professional career, I have begun with enthusiasm about my new opportunity—and in every case, what first felt like an inspiring opportunity turned into a personally and organizationally difficult job.

Was this normal? Was it supposed to be? Is it necessary to go through life accepting that working is difficult, that it brings challenges that don't feel good, and that this is the reality we must live with for most of our adult lives?

There were some messages I refused to accept, like:

"In order to succeed, I need to establish a career."

"In order to establish a career, I need to make others and particularly my boss like me (more than they like others)."

"I need to do a good job (in the eyes of others and particularly of my boss)."

"If things don't work as planned or intended, there will need to be someone to blame (hopefully not me)."

I deeply disliked these messages and the underlying story about my own inability to have integrity in a system that sapped my enthusiasm and tried to replace it with extrinsic motivation. Even when I was the "boss", as CEO of both my family company and a startup that I simultaneously founded and led, I still felt burdened by the dynamic. I didn't know a better way, so I kept grinding away.

The day came when I couldn't grind any longer, so I stepped out of both companies and founded my own boutique consultancy. Surely working with individuals and organizations interested in changing power dynamics would set me free from the old stories, right? I was excited and passionate about this work, and for years I coached and consulted with organizations ranging from three-person teams to businesses with tens of thousands of employees. I found I could connect beautifully with the people in my workshops and with my coaching clients, I learned a lot more about power dynamics in organizations of all sizes, and I saw the effects of our system on people at all levels of the power hierarchy. I received a strong influx of positive feedback and repeat business. People loved my workshops and left feeling inspired—and for years, this was enough to support me in feeling like a success.

Several years in, I began to observe that despite the rave reviews, the data didn't support assumptions about the effectiveness of my work. Instead, more often than not, my clients went back to their everyday work lives and organizational dynamics pulled them back into the same old patterns. While my work might have inspired one person or one team, it wasn't making a difference systemically. Even a combination of organization development and leadership development failed to yield lasting results.

My services were labeled as "change management", which in most cases meant that people high up in the power hierarchy were making a structural change, and engaging my leadership training in hopes that it would equip managers with tools to deal with the huge amount of frustration those change management processes triggered. Ultimately, I realized that my achievements were more about minimizing frustration than about contributing to whole system improvement.

This realization piqued my curiosity. What stood in the way of really meaningful change? What was missing? With all my years of experience as an employee, as a founder and CEO, and as a consultant and coach, I realized that the need was much, much bigger—it was a call for a fundamentally new way of understanding our systems and ourselves.

Against the wall

By 2009, when I was coming to this realization, a valued colleague and good friend had joined my company as a partner and we both felt the drive that all entrepreneurs feel: to find a better way! While neither of us knew what it was that needed to shift so fundamentally, we went searching. What we found was Holacracy.

It was fascinating to step into this really new world. My friend and I were enthusiastic, and so excited. Without really understanding (yet) what it meant to shift into this totally new way of organizing, we went for it—big time. The promise of "a whole scale replacement of the management hierarchy" and "a system of distributed authority" was almost too good to be true. We started implementing this practice ourselves and also offering public workshops.

It's important to note that at that time, terms like "self-organization" were known only to people who were deep into systems theory. "Distributed authority" was jargon that few people could define in the context of business and organization, and "purpose" usually triggered discussion of the seemingly inalienable fact that the ultimate purpose of a business is to make money. It's inspiring to think how far we have come in a little over a decade, but we'll get there later.

After only a few months of practicing, things got really difficult for my business partner and me. We kept running into problems when it came to practicing Holacracy. I wish I knew then what I know now, but of course hindsight is 20/20. Our conflicts grew. I was "all in", trying to practice by the rules of the Holacracy Constitution. She needed something different, something I didn't understand. The situation frustrated the hell out of both of us and I think we both felt let down by the other. Shifting our way of organizing had driven our business, our business partnership, and our friendship against the wall.

It was my first and most painful experience of something that seems so clear now in retrospect: when you shift into a fundamentally different dynamic of doing work together, it isn't just the practices, the rules, and processes that change. The people change, too, and I dare say that at the time nobody knew what the depth of this transformation really meant for the human beings involved.

At the time, lacking the consciousness and the tools to deal with our conflicts, my colleague and I parted ways. She left the company, and sadly our friendship never recovered from this experience.

Endings and new beginnings

The dissolution of this friendship and business partnership was quite a loss—however, it was also the beginning of a journey that brought me to writing this book. This was one of my first opportunities to observe a pattern, one I've witnessed again and again while accompanying people and organizations on their journey of implementing Holacracy. This pattern can be summed up through one big question, called out by many, over and over again: "What about the people?".

When researching other offerings like Sociocracy, Conscious Business, Responsive, Teal (a movement following Frederic Laloux's book *Reinventing Organizations*), and others, I observed two phenomena:

1. There was (and is) an ever-growing desire to shift the way we do work together, globally, in every type of organization that exists.

2. Every single offering of a new way to organize triggers its own problems for the people involved.

Most of the offerings are too "people" oriented, which triggered the organizations to fall back into conventional "power over" dynamics. This creates confusion and huge disappointment for the people involved. Holacracy, with its clarity around "governing the organization, not the people", offers a system that promises to fully distribute authority and that at the same time very often causes a lot of pain, leaving people suffering from insecurity, feeling alienated from their colleagues, and experiencing the workplace as having moved into a cold, impersonal state.

One question fascinated me: why, on the one hand, is there so much pain and struggle involved, while on the other hand, there is such a deep need and longing for a shift? It is clear that people believe in the value of finding new ways of engaging, both individually and collectively, in order to be of better service to people and planet, and yet somehow there is an almost insurmountable obstacle for many attempting this shift. I became aware that in order to seriously explore and connect to my question, I had to begin with my own struggles and pains.

Why change the way we organize?

Many wonderful authors have written great books to explore this question. These titles help many readers orient themselves to what seems to be going on globally in our times. In my own quest to satisfy my curiosity about new ways of working, I read book after book and in everyone there was so much for me to learn. Nonetheless I continued to feel that I was missing something . . . that there was something more, just out of reach. Still dissatisfied, I decided to shift more consciously into *beginner's mind*: a state of not knowing. Deciding to begin with myself, I tried to cultivate a quality of open curiosity, without prejudgment. I asked, at the deepest, most meaningful level, "why is it so important *to me* that I personally contribute to shifting the way we people collectively organize?"

Selection of Books on the New World of Work

Frederic Laloux: *Reinventing Organizations: A Guide to Creating Organizations Inspired by the Next Stage in Human Consciousness*; Nelson Parker; 1st edition (February 10, 2014)

Brian J. Robertson: *Holacracy: The New Management System for a Rapidly Changing World*; Henry Holt and Co. (June 2, 2015)

> Selection of Books on the New World of Work (continued)
>
> Ted J. Rauh, Jerry Koch-Gonzalez: *Many Voices One Song: Shared Power With Sociocracy*; Institute for Peaceable Communities, Inc; Illustrated edition (June 11, 2018)
>
> Aaron Dignan: *Brave New Work: Are You Ready to Reinvent Your Organization?* Portfolio; Illustrated edition (February 19, 2019)
>
> Doug Kirkpatrick: *The No-Limits Enterprise: Organizational Self-Management In The New World Of Work*; ForbesBooks (July 23, 2019)
>
> Jo Aschenbrenner: *The For-Purpose Enterprise: A Powershifted Operating System to Run Your Business*; tredition (November 2, 2020)
>
> Marco Robledo: 3D Management, an Integral Theory for Organizations in the Vanguard of Evolution; Cambridge Scholars Publishing (April 26, 2021)

Viewing this question with openness and curiosity allowed me to see aspects of my own yearning as they were expressing themselves globally—in relation to our profound collective pain; our cumulative human wisdom; and the potential in our species' journey.

Collective Pain

There is so much pain. We humans, in an increasingly interconnected world, are aware of so much of it: Poverty, hunger, mental and physical sickness, injustice, inequity, hate, war, maltreatment of animals, depletion of our natural resources, environmental devastation, and more.

As we sit with this reality, questions arise: How much pain is part of life? How much pain have we learned to simply accept as part of life? How much pain do we feel empowered to transcend, and what is holding us back from doing so?

Collective Wisdom

We as a species have so much wisdom. We have been on our planet for approximately 6 million years, and have gone through and survived so much. The richness and diversity of human wisdom is unimaginable.

As we soak in this truth, we might ask: How much wisdom are we consciously accessing? How much wisdom have we lost on the way? How much wisdom are we ignoring? How much wisdom are we hiding? What is holding us back from accessing and using the depth and breadth of wisdom that is accessible to us?

Collective Journey

This moment in our collective journey holds so much potential. We humans are always exploring and expressing life's possibilities. This creative exploration is what makes us grow and develop, and what accounts for the many different ways we live our lives and organize our societies.

This potential can inspire questions in us: Why have we grown to see so many things as separate? Why do we divide, label, and categorize things as we do, for better or for worse? Are the lenses through which we view the world helpful or harmful? Why have we lost our sense of connection to the greater whole, the web of life[2]? Was this loss accidental or purposeful? What is holding us back from feeling the connectedness of everything?

Numerous initiatives point towards three global challenges—the challenge of ending pain, the challenge of sourcing wisdom,

---

[2] Fritjof Capra: *The Web of Life: A New Scientific Understanding of Living Systems*; Anchor; 8/16/97 edition (September 15, 1997)

and the challenge of realizing potential. Each invites us to engage our life energy, one way or another, in order to make things better. Books are written, communities emerge and grow, conferences and workshops reach millions of people. For the first time in human history, technology enables us to reach out to every corner of the earth with our endeavors and we see common efforts rippling through nations around the globe.

Explorations of power

The "New World of Work" is a global movement with tremendous potential for far-reaching impact. Whatever we humans intend to do together, organizing ourselves is one of the first steps toward doing it. For this reason, organizing is the most powerful force humanity has developed to reach desired outcomes. Think of the power of organizing in a standard hierarchy, where one person in a position of power can initiate billions of dollars in financial transactions or authorize deadly airstrikes halfway around the globe; or the power of grassroots organizing, which has rewoven the social fabric of many communities and nations, including but not limited to South Africa, the United States, and India.

The power hierarchy is the most common way of organizing today, and it has completely defined our collective story about how to organize. The pyramid of power is an incredible success story of humanity and therefore still is the most widely adopted organizing system. It has helped us expedite innovation in all aspects of our lives. And it has eventually become self-serving to an extent that it is incapable of seeing the harm it is creating parallel to its usefulness.

Our ways of organizing shape every aspect of our lives. Over time we have created highly successful ways of organizing, and through effective organizing we have begun to accumulate power. Eventually humans learned how to consciously create systems that utilize power in service of the desired outcomes, continuously refining it for ever increasing effectiveness and efficiency—these are the systems that allow a single person, or the occupants of a single boardroom, to trigger those billion-dollar transactions and those deadly strikes.

These examples show us that somewhere along the way, our common way of organizing became less about impact and outcome, and more about power itself—about using power to increase power.

Power through currency

Humanity created a system called "money" for itself, originally as a fair value exchange for things that meet our needs. From there, money has grown to be the currency of power. We have learned to believe that rich equals powerful, while poor equals powerless. This is a story so entrenched in our society that we forget money's simple roots, as a fair value exchange for goods, time, or labor, and instead value it as an indicator of power. Today, money often rewards behaviors that ignore the common good or, even worse, act contrary to our collective wellbeing and even survival.

Power through systemic education

Do you believe knowledge is power? Or do you believe that those with access to knowledge, or those with access to degrees or certificates indicating educational status, have greater access to opportunities than those lacking an academic education? We have learned to believe that education is about gaining knowledge in order to become successful. Returning to the question of currency, our cultures tend to equate being successful with being wealthy and/or influential. Ultimately, today, education is less about igniting the fire of curiosity and self-expression in one another, and more about preparing select individuals to gain access to power.

New Stories of Love, Power, and Purpose

Power through identity

Race is not a biological but a social construct[3], and yet it has become a powerful indicator of one's likelihood to succeed in many of our hierarchical systems. During a period of Western European expansion and colonialism, the story of race was born, and it now threads deeply through the roots of systemic inequity in many of our nations. Likewise, identities like gender, class, culture of origin, and others shape the likelihood of one's being hired at a firm, receiving a promotion or pay raise, or even surviving into old age!

The loss of connection makes power dysfunctional

The list goes on—nearly every system within which we are navigating today is about power. Power, in itself, is not a bad thing—but when power becomes self-serving, and is used to increase itself, that's when it loses connection to everything else. It is that loss of connection that leads to power becoming dysfunctional.

Much as money, education, and even our relationship with the planet itself has become about power, organizing in so many cases has become about power for power's sake. Organizing is at the core of all systems, and the power hierarchy serves to organize power in almost every human institution. Moving up a "career ladder" is about becoming more powerful. We call it "success" and success is rewarded in so many ways: money, status, and admiration, just to name a few.

A lot of research has been conducted on the influence of power on our brain. What we see there is troubling.[4] Research shows that power, when understood and embodied as "power over", increases behavior guided by self-interest, decreases compassion, and can

---

[3] "There is no such thing as race. None. Scientifically, anthropologically, racism is a construct - a social construct." From Reesma Menakem: "My Grandmother's Hands: Racialized Trauma and the Pathway to Mending Our Hearts and Bodies"; Central Recovery Press (21 Aug. 2017)

[4] https://www.theatlantic.com/magazine/archive/2017/07/power-causes-brain-damage/528711/?utm_source

even rewire the brain. "Power, in fact, impairs a specific neural process, 'mirroring,' that may be a cornerstone of empathy," writes Jerry Useem, reporting on the research of Sukhvinder Obhi.

In an article Marwa Azab, Ph.D., in *Psychology Today*[5], we're told that, "the brains of powerful individuals react differently to social cues in ways that resemble psychopaths or patients with frontal brain damage. Psychopaths and some patients with brain damage lack empathy and the ability to take others' perspectives. Research has shown that power can deform the brain to act in the same ways. For example, people with high status have been shown to be less accurate in judging the emotions of people with low status."

In light of the growing, global needs for community, compassion, and embodied interconnectedness if we are to face the challenges of our times, it becomes increasingly clear: the old story of power is ceasing to be useful. We need a new story of what power is and how it can be of service to the greater whole.

Pathways for organizing

When I first started delivering public workshops on self-organization, distributed authority, and purpose-guided business over a decade ago, the most common argument brought up against it was that business was about making money. Since nine out of ten participants would agree, I had to learn not to get dragged into a discussion about whether this assumption was right or wrong, but rather to take a "yes, and" approach before explaining other ways of looking at our approaches, and purposes, for organizing.

Today, thankfully, more and more people are able to appreciate the value created by organizations and businesses, and how they create positive impacts on a scale unlike any seen before. They are

---

[5] https://www.psychologytoday.com/us/blog/neuroscience-in-everyday-life/202006/the-brain-under-the-influence-power;

also able to see how many organizations and businesses consolidate power in the hands of the few. They see the danger in this phenomenon, as some organizations and businesses nourish greed, inequity, disconnection, and destruction through their very ways of being.

In recognizing the power of organizing and the dangers of these toxic outcomes, many people are awakening to the amazing potential that lies in changing the way we do work together.

Explorations of the New World of Work

New ways of organizing have been explicitly named in Western cultures since at least the late 1950s, when W.L. Gore began to rethink management and leadership. In the 1970s Gerhard Endenburg in The Netherlands defined Sociocracy and in the early 1980s, Ricardo Semler innovated with Semco in Brazil. These are just a few of the most famous pioneers of what we call "The New World of Work".

Today, this movement is huge. In 2007, Holacracy followed Sociocracy, marketing itself as the first full scale replacement for the management hierarchy. Agile and Scrum moved from software approaches to whole system solutions, and the Teal movement followed Frederic Laloux's book *Reinventing Organizations*. Responsive Org, Conscious Business, DAOs, the For-Purpose Enterprise, the Symbiotic Enterprise, and other initiatives around decentralization were innovated and launched. It is impossible to make a complete list of new approaches, as it is getting longer each day. This is a global movement, continuously growing, and it is not going away. It is calling out loudly: *The power hierarchy has run its course!*

The wonderful new forms of organizing that have merged over the last decade and a half have many differences and some similarities, and each has something unique to offer. They have one thing in common: they all intend to offer solutions for phenomena that have been showing up and rapidly growing all over the world for many years. These phenomena include disengagement, burnout, and depression despite—or perhaps as a result of—management and leadership practices geared towards ever increasing efficiency and effectiveness. Today we even have a name for the consequence of these phenomena. It's called "The Great Resignation"[6]. All this is fueling the global need for change.

For obvious reasons, new approaches to work are geared towards creating more humane work conditions so that our jobs might nourish our hearts and souls rather than sucking every bit of energy out of us. In doing so, and in one way or another, each of the "New Work" approaches addresses the issue of power.

What's missing?

In all the years that I have been focused on the shift into new forms of organizing, I have seen certain, interrelated phenomena that show up again and again, and seem to indicate a movement-wide "blind spot". What follows are a few examples where 21st century forms of organizing, or at least attempts at them, have led to people and organizations suffering as much, or more, than before the transition from standard power hierarchy. Each is defined in generalizations but represents a scenario I've encountered repeatedly.

Case Study: Implicit power takes control

The hierarchy was (almost) kicked out, while the top management (the remaining hierarchy) declared the organization to be flat. Employees were then asked to self-organize, which gave the term self-organization the following meaning: "Do what you think is right and organize yourself, either alone or with others, so that the work gets done". This created a lot of confusion, insecurity, and pain and led to an implicit, unofficial power hierarchy taking over. This pushed the downsides of a power hierarchy—the unhealthy

---

[6] https://en.wikipedia.org/wiki/Great_Resignation;

"power over" dynamics—into shadow, as the lack of both structure and agreed upon processes for decision making left a big void. This void then got filled by an implicit/unofficial power structure, held by people who were better at "playing the power over game" than others. Everybody's initial high expectations of more personal freedom and self-directed working ended in disappointment, with increasing interpersonal conflicts arising as a result of the informal, unspoken power hierarchy.

Case Study: Human Resources at the helm

The CEO and top management declared, "we are going Teal!" The Human Resources department was asked to manage and navigate the change. Normally, HR professionals are highly interested in providing people in the organization with what they need to be content in the workplace, while at the same time navigating the mostly bureaucratic employment needs of the organization. The HR department had neither the tools for something that was so completely new nor clear direction about how to manage this change. "Going Teal" was defined as, "read the book (Frederic Laloux's 'Reinventing Organizations') and do it." Everyone involved experienced confusion and lack of orienting support. As a result, expectations were dashed—the employees' expectations of more flexibility, freedom, and personal purpose-alignment in their work, as well as managers' expectations of increased engagement and productivity. This led to a lot of disappointment and frustration. The HR professionals were broadly accused of doing a bad job and failing to manage the transition.

Case Study: No more bosses

The CEO and top management decided to shift the organization through implementing a new management system that promised to distribute authority. This was met with euphoria, and the promise of the power hierarchy being kicked out. "No more bosses" was the big promise, and people got excited. Soon, however, people began to feel cut off. They experienced their workplace as cold and impersonal. Plus, because of the personal development journey that this transition called for, people felt overwhelmed, scared, and alone.

Newly introduced processes that were designed to support engaged and autonomous work got tedious and stuck. Confusion and conflict entered as people tried to deal with work issues without seeing a channel to address hopes and fears, relational tensions, and other matters pertaining to people and feelings. These personal and interpersonal issues stood in the way of work getting done and kept processes from working as intended. Soon, despite the high hopes and lofty expectations of many involved, the function of the organization slowed to a crawl.

As in many other cases, this led to the CEO falling back into his typical old role behaviors, tossing aside what had become tedious new processes and taking up an informal "management" role without the explicit authority to do so.

Case Study: The guinea pig department

A large corporation decided to test new forms of organizing. The top management chose the IT department to be the "guinea pig", to prototype the new form and see how it worked. People in the department went through euphoria, into struggle and frustration. Navigating the boundaries to the otherwise conventional organization was difficult, but people held on, somehow seeing the value this shift could bring. Then, before new skills were firmly grounded, the top management decided that this experiment was taking too long. Seeing the struggles and frustrations in the IT department, the management declared the test a failure.

Case Study: The guinea pig department (alternate ending)

In another case, HR was the "guinea pig" department. Things were moving forward, with euphoria, struggle, and frustrations raising their heads at the appropriate moments. Then, a new CEO joined the organization. Seeing this strange cell within the system, and learning that this cell had a boundary within which they had no direct control, the new boss immediately declared the test as ended and ordered the department to go back to "normal" structures and processes.

Both "guinea pig" cases left people in a really difficult situation. We can't unlearn what we have learned. While some people were relieved by these decisions, most were frustrated and lost in the middle of things. They learned to do one of two things: swallow their disappointment and return to old organizing systems or leave the jobs that they had otherwise enjoyed.

Other examples: the non-profit shadow

In non-profit and non-governmental organizations, the people involved are generally intentionally purpose driven. In general, these organizations are driven to improve something in their communities, countries, or world, sometimes relating to huge social and environmental problems. Over the years I have observed connected phenomena which I call "the non-profit shadow".

People working for these organizations generally like to work in a way that feels good to everybody—they are by nature inspired to find ways that are collaborative, egalitarian, empowered, and meaningful. The history of nonprofits, socially conditioned behaviors, and the financial and legal conditions of non-profits lead to something very different: people in this industry tend to be overworked and underpaid, while power struggles between the operational staff and the board of directors are often energy drainers. Most endeavors of non-profits or NGOs to move towards self-organization with distributed authority fail because of the resistance of the board and the power structure it represents.

As in the case studies above, an attempt to move into New Work in the non-profit sector often ends in pain and frustrations. Here it is particularly difficult for the people involved, as everybody cares so much about the purpose of the organization. Many non-profit staff members don't want to leave and would much rather hold the pain. These wonderful people stick to doing the work they are passionate about, even when their working environments drain them of huge amounts of energy.

Deep unlearning and new learning

Is it really necessary for deep change into a new paradigm to be accompanied by so much pain, frustration, and wasted effort? While I believe the answer is a resounding, "no!", the solution is not a silver bullet. The capacity-building of both people and systems takes time and deliberate nurturing.

For organizations going through large-scale change, it is normal and even necessary for work to slow down. Then, as productivity and financial outputs decrease, it's normal for resistance to the change to take root in people and grow. While people in systems undergoing such change need new skills and new approaches to organizing work, they also need pathways to manage their expectations and process their feelings.

In the field of Change Management, we know to give this issue a lot of attention—however, even experienced change managers are used to working within power hierarchies. The power hierarchy gives some sense of control and the certainty that when things get tough, someone has the ultimate power to make decisions and dictate what should happen next. This can have the effect of decreasing uncertainty and fear—with someone in the driver's seat, people feel taken care of.

In this New World of Work, this is precisely what we intend to move away from. In a world where people have been socialized to look for the one in charge, taking away the paternal function of the power hierarchy and its power holding actors can leave a gap. This missing power-holding figure(s) creates as much—or, because of the completely different nature of the shift, even more—insecurity and fear than in any earlier change.

In almost all cases of moving away from the power hierarchy, the one thing most frequently underestimated is the need for deep unlearning and new learning, leading to a mind shift of the people—all people—involved, and the amount of focus and time this requires. This process happens in different ways and requires very different time spans for each person involved, as we are all so different. The consequences of this underestimation can be harsh.

Some consequences of underestimating the necessary mind shift:

- **Disappointment** and **frustration**, if the former leaders haven't yet quite stepped into shifting power and start falling back into old patterns of controlling and (micro) managing—often, out of pure concern for the organization and the responsibility they are used to holding.

- **Resistance** in those who need more time, fueled by the atmosphere of judgment that can be created when some people have been able to adapt and integrate the new way of working faster than others, lack of understanding for those who need more time, and feel held back by them.

- **Fear,** stemming from **insecurity**, among people who don't have the confidence that they can do a good job in a system that functions so totally differently. The change we are talking about here is bigger than any change people have been invited to go through ever before. Going far beyond a simple structural change, this change—as mentioned before—requires a huge shift of mindset and requires us to let go of beliefs we have been holding for most of our lives and that have served us well in conventional work settings.

- **Psychological pain** and sometimes even **trauma** can result when people fear losing their jobs in the face of so much that is new. The need for psychological safety is immense and very often there are no possibilities to create the conditions for this safety. The threat to one's livelihood can feel very real when our employment conditions shift so dramatically.

- **Conflict** between and **conflation** of the needs of the people and the needs of the organization can result in the **system losing power**. Due to conflation, decision making processes often go around in repeated efforts to integrate personal concerns, which has a slowing effect on things that actually need to move forward. This can be frustrating regardless of whether people feel that their needs are *prioritized* by the new way of working, or whether they feel that their needs are *insufficiently represented* due to structural changes.

- **Rejection** and **disregard** for the perspectives of those who embrace the new system, especially when some managers have not yet integrated these possibilities and are still grounded in the conventional control mindset. In many systems, those who see the value in the learning opportunity and the possibility of autonomy and agency in the new system begin to develop the empowered expression that's invited and enabled by the new form of organizing and are then shut down by former power holders. Being penalized for using one's voice can be painful and can trigger frustration, anger, and fear—a destructive emotion that always gets in the way of personal growth.

It's important to note that we are still in the early days of New Work—the movement is like a toddler, eager to develop the capacity to walk freely and steadily, but not quite there. Elements of the power hierarchy look at the toddler and ask, "can't you grow up to be more like me?" But you know what? This is not going away, and it is not devolving into the same old system we're used to. This is growing, and it is growing fast. The web of life is calling for it.

2

Everything is Connected

I don't know exactly when, why, or how, but at some point, meditation became a part of my life. I only know that it entered my life quietly, then left and came back a few times before it was there to stay. I vividly remember the moment when it finally returned to my life for good.

Presence and mindfulness were becoming increasingly popular in the world of consulting and coaching during the first decade of this century. Being perpetually curious, I joined a retreat entitled, "Mindfulness in Systemic Coaching and Consulting". The context was crucial to my experience. The retreat was set in a former monastery that had become a special place combining eastern and western wisdom and spiritual traditions. The vegetarian food, cooked in Zen practice, tasted so wonderful that every act of eating was a sensual joy. Meals were taken in silence, which for me was unusual. Prior to this retreat, I had considered meal times in a group setting to be a time of sharing experiences and getting to know each other better. Surprisingly, the quality of the time spent together during these silent meals touched me deeply.

We spent a lot of time sitting in meditation during the retreat—then, something happened.

I hardly have the words to describe the life changing experience that I had. Here's the best I can offer: at one point in a meditation, my sense of self—my whole being—began to expand. It expanded, expanded, and expanded, until everything shifted. I experienced myself as a part of it all, connected to everything . . . big and small at the same time, there with it all, now and forever.

Again, I hardly have the words to describe what it was like. I only know that it changed my life. Nothing was the same from that moment on.

At first, I was overwhelmed by the experience, and I tried to understand what had happened. Eventually, I let go of trying to understand it cognitively. This made room for tremendous gratitude. I feel so gifted to have had this experience. I haven't had it again, though I meditate regularly. Though I don't expect it to happen again, it remains present with me. Nothing in this world or beyond can take the experience away from me. It is me.

It also gave direction to my quest for understanding the blind spots in the world of New Work.

Have you had the experience of deciding to buy something that gives you joy, when suddenly you begin to see that same thing everywhere? A dog, a wristwatch, a car, a backpack . . . whatever it is, once something good has come to your attention you will begin to see more of it around. That's what happened to me. An endless stream of books, articles, podcasts, and videos about presence, mindfulness, and the connectedness of everything began to enter my awareness.

Books - Important companions on this part of my journey:

Ken Wilber: *A Theory of Everything: An Integral Vision for Business, Politics, Science and Spirituality*; Shambhala; Later prt. edition (October 16, 2001)

Ken Wilber: *Integral Life Practice: A 21st-Century Blueprint for Physical Health, Emotional Balance, Mental Clarity, and Spiritual Awakening*; Integral Books; Illustrated edition (September 9, 2008)

Eckhard Tolle: *The Power of Now: A Guide to Spiritual Enlightenment*; New World Library (August 1, 2004)

Byron Katie and Stephen Mitchell: *Loving What Is: Four Questions That Can Change Your Life*; Three Rivers Press; Reprint edition (December 23, 2003)

Byron Katie and Stephen Mitchell: *A Thousand Names For Joy: Living in Harmony with the Way Things Are*; Harmony; 3.2.2008 edition (April 1, 2008)

Peter Senge, Otto Scharmer, Joseph Jaworski, Betty Sue Flowers: *Presence: Human Purpose and the Field of the Future*; Society for Organizational Learning (March 1, 2004)

Daniel J. Siegel: *Mindsight; The New Science of Personal Transformation*; Bantam; Reprint edition (December 28, 2010)

Rupert Spira: *Presence (Volume 1): The Art of Peace and Happiness; Presence (Volume 2): The Intimacy of all Experience*; Sahaja; Second Edition, Revised (December 1, 2016)

Thich Nhat Hanh: *The Miracle of Mindfulness; An Introduction to the Practice of Meditation*; Beacon Press; 1st edition (May 1, 1999)

> Books - Important companions on this part of my journey (continued):
>
> Thich Nhat Hanh: *You Are Here: Discovering the Magic of the Present Moment*; Shambhala; Reprint edition (December 21, 2010)
>
> Condensing the works of the many beautiful authors and teachers from whom I have learned to the few on this list means leaving out others. Knowing that a list can never be complete, I bow in gratitude to these wisdom-keepers as well as to those I have not named.

My profound experience of oneness during meditation helped me understand, on the level of my soul, how I am a part of everything, and everything is a part of me. My words for this always seem so small, so insignificant to me, because I simply cannot find any different way of saying it. Thankfully others have expressed this in wonderful ways, so I am grateful and relieved that I can point towards the book list shared above.

The human cost of the race for success

Why is the understanding of the connectedness of everything so important for the shift in how we humans collectively organize?

Most human endeavors—companies, organizations, businesses and enterprises—are, at their heart, intended to serve society with what it needs. Over the 20th Century, we have learned to turn these endeavors into systems of high efficiency and effectiveness.

In itself, serving society with efficiency and effectiveness is a wonderful thing. Over time, however, and at such a slow pace as to be almost unrecognized, the general intention of many of these endeavors to serve society shifted to the intention of serving themselves. Profit, and the wellbeing of those few that benefited most from it, became the focus of our endeavors' efficiency and effectiveness. Measures like sustainability, community and social benefit, and environmental impact, though increasingly called for, are deprioritized to efficiency and effectiveness in service of financial success and thus become lip service.

Fueled by our capitalistic system, which depends on never-ending growth, the idea of "enough" had to be erased and substituted by "there is never enough" in order to justify the dynamics of creating needs. This happened through the promise of happiness of all kinds through material goods. The need for continuous growth led economic dynamics to manipulate us—now "consumers"—into a continuous sense of scarcity, with the ongoing promise of "when/then". "When you can afford this, then you will be happy. When you have reached 'this' or 'that', then you will be happy." Life became a never-ending race for happiness, promised through material possession.

We see this playing out in fashion (new every season, if not more often), cars, jewelry, travel, and of course all the products that make us more beautiful, younger, thinner, fitter, or cleverer. Each of these aspirations gives root to huge industries based on stories of how we need to be different from how we actually are. When we live with the dictate of "when/then", nothing can ever be enough, and life becomes an ongoing rat race for the "then". This creates an omnipresent sense of scarcity.

In his book *Sacred Economics: Money, Gift, and Society in the Age of Transition*[7], Charles Eisenstein describes how this sense of scarcity plays out for us:

> "When everything is subject to money, then the scarcity of money makes everything scarce, including the basis of human life and happiness. Such is the life of the slave—one whose actions are compelled by threat to survival."

---

[7] http://sacred-economics.com/wp-content/uploads/2012/01/sacred-economics-book-text.pdf

Part of this rat race is the race for success, rewarded by a) money, and b) power, which both bring c) status. All three can, and often do, create addiction.[8]

What happens to our brain when we get addicted? We develop an overwhelming need to have our fix. Not having access to it, or experiencing the loss of it, is unbearable. We become willing to do things we otherwise would never do in order to make sure we always have it.

The organizational system of the power hierarchy that has been so successful (efficient and effective) in the business world for more than a century has the rewards of money, power, and status built into it. It simply doesn't function without these three drivers. We are told that happiness comes through being successful in this way. If we don't achieve that, we are a failure. May the games begin.

To participate, we enter an organization and are sucked into a system that creates addiction. Yet, by nature we are not wired for addiction to make us happy. We are wired for happiness through meaning, relationships, and well-being. While on the surface, we tag along and play by the rules, more and more of us begin to become aware of this part inside of us that resists the game—that tries to fight against it. This fight results, for many, in symptoms like depression, burn out, dysfunctional relationships, high blood pressure, and other stress-related health issues.

All these sad results that we are seeing as increasing phenomena in our society are the result of the stories of separateness that have become the makeup of our belief system. Stories of independence, individuality, and worth defined by personal achievements deny the reality that we are social beings in a complex society and a fundamentally interconnected planet and universe.

My meditative experience of connection, described above, allowed me to question my belief systems in a completely new way. On this never-ending journey of exploration, I have reached

---

[8] https://blog.politics.ox.ac.uk/neurochemistry-power-implications-political-change/
https://rivierarecovery.com/money-addiction-does-it-exist/

a point where I say that I believe—not just cognitively, but with every fiber of my being and becoming—that everything is connected and interdependent; there is "Interbeing", as Thích Nhất Hạnh calls it and as Charles Eisenstein further explores in his book *The More Beautiful World Our Heart Knows Is Possible*. Everything is connected in the web of life.

This new story changed my perspective on everything. It changed how I want to live my everyday life, how I want to do and perceive my work, and how I want to be in relationship with myself, with others, and with everything.

When this realization first dawned on me, I knew that the work I was doing at the time was not an expression of my inner journey. I felt detached from what I was doing, which of course was the exact opposite of what I wanted for my life. I faced a big new question: *how can the connectedness of everything be the foundational principle on which everything we do in our collective endeavors is based?* This is the question that brought me to self-organization.

The blossoming of a movement

It has been fascinating to watch how the movement toward "the New World of Work" has blossomed like a meadow in spring with its variety of different flowers. Some bold pioneers, as mentioned before, have been looking for different ways to organize work since the 1950s, and on their shoulders more and more businesses and movements have emerged to offer supposed solutions. Many are still caught up in the dynamics of asking, "which answer is the best?".

I admit, I have also been part of this general excitement of finding the "best answer". I was drawn immediately into Holacracy when I learned about it and began to practice it and introduce it to client organizations. I was highly motivated by the shift it represented. In my very thorough search for alternatives that would help me connect my work with my learnings, Holacracy was the only answer I found that served as a true alternative to the power hierarchy.

My practice with Holacracy was a steep learning journey, and it gave me the first glimpse of what it can actually mean to shift into the principle of the connectedness of everything. Very soon, however, I realized that it wasn't the answer I was looking for. Though it was, and continues to be, a very important part of the New Work movement, there was something deeply missing.

While many felt something missing and turned away from Holacracy, I took a different approach. A response of "yes, and . . ." allowed me to continue my search without dismissing what I had learned. Integrating my learning and highly appreciating Holacracy for what it had to offer, I continued to seek additional pieces without rejecting Holacracy for its place in the puzzle.

Since about 2010, and throughout the movement, more and more answers and offerings have emerged. In conjunction, confusion around different terminology increased. Self-Organization, Self-Management, Agile, Scrum, Teal, Responsive, Conscious, People Centric, and many other terms emerged to describe different ways to go about organizing work together in new ways.

While the movement was evolving, and I was evolving my understanding along with it, I was personally struggling with a sense of being stuck. I continued to coach and consult, focused on implementing Holacracy with client organizations, while struggling inwardly with an almost indescribable feeling of potential—something was there, yet just out of sight. I had a feeling that I was missing something, yet I couldn't precisely name what that something was. This left me feeling judgmental, and unable to connect my work to the feeling I had personally experienced through meditation. My deep experience of the connectedness of everything couldn't connect to "the world out there", and I came to a new question: *what is the connection between my inner world and the outer expression of my work in the world?*

Voices of intuition

I realized I was faced with a paradox. On the one hand, the connectedness of everything had become a life-guiding principle for me, while on the other hand I needed to differentiate my own thinking from that of others in search of clarity.

This dilemma brought me to a crucial realization. It brought me into direct confrontation with some of my personal patterns, some deep shadows that I'd been previously unaware of. I had to consciously face these patterns and transcend them before I could move on. This period of self-exploration was difficult for me, but it did allow me to shift into a new form of listening to and trusting my inner voices.

During this period, I began to journal regularly. This helped me dive into a whole new level of exploring and learning. Today I have a fully developed daily journaling practice (called JournaLogue) that has not only helped me but has also helped many of my clients to navigate their own journey of learning and personal growth. I'll refer to the JournaLogue again throughout the book, then detail the practice in Chapter 6 so that you can practice it and adopt the aspects of it that are supportive for your personal journey.

Through this journaling practice, I found a way of searching for clarity that included my rational thinking, but also so much more. I learned to trust my voices of intuition. Grounded in the understanding that I am a part of everything, I realized that what emerged through me could only come through, and from, this connectedness.

In the chapters that follow, you'll hear accounts of my journey through an inner and interconnected world—including the companions, or parts of my psyche, that have come to accompany me on my journey of soul discovery through the JournaLogue practice. This has brought deep, meaningful, and often surprising information to my awareness and has supported me in my ongoing learning and growth.

One discovery, made through this process, was that the most important terminology that was guiding my work—whether in conversations or in books and articles—was used in many different ways and loaded with often conflicting meanings. The top terms on that list were self-organization, self-management, leadership, and power. Without solid, shared understanding of the meanings of these terms, experts and practitioners could never arrive at collective understanding and readiness to move forward.

I realized that before developing my JournaLogue practice, my quest for meaning had been focused on the outside—on reading, listening, watching, and trying to make sense of others' perspectives. When it came to the professional part of my life, I had been living a form of separation. My professional learning had been mainly guided by my rational mind, while my personal development journey had been guided from within.

My JournaLogue practice helped me close that gap. My quest wasn't an either/or anymore, but an "all in". I was learning to access all possible available resources, both outside and within myself. Through this shift I could follow my curiosity on all different levels—mind, body, heart, and spirit. With this new understanding, rather than trying to make total sense, I began to explore the space between—to view things through their connections rather than the other way around.

I finally understood how self-organization had been keeping me in its spell. I had felt as though it wanted me to keep searching until I saw something, and here it was: self-organization was not a term describing how we organize our enterprises, but the organizing principle of the connectedness of everything—the web of life, the greater whole. The reality struck me profoundly:

Self-organization is the evolutionary principle of the universe.

The evolutionary principle of the universe

Since its beginning, the web of life has evolved—continuously growing into ever more complexity—through self-organization.

New Stories of Love, Power, and Purpose

Based on this understanding, self-organizing our enterprises means that we mirror and break down these organizing principles into a form that we humans can master. What this makes possible is astonishing—our success in this endeavor means that our enterprises have the potential to tune into and dance along with the evolutionary rhythm of the universe, and the web of life.

Self-organizing enterprises as a whole now can sense into that web, and from that sense of "Interbeing" respond accordingly. This makes it possible for every human and every collective endeavor to find its unique place in the web of life, in service of the greater whole. This unique place from where we serve the greater whole defines purpose.

The journey to this holistic understanding invites us to let go of old belief systems that have been guiding humanity for a very long time and that are deeply ingrained in the stories we tell ourselves. We are now called to develop new stories. Instead of trying to predict and control an outcome, we can learn to be present in the moment, sense into what is needed, sense what wants to emerge, and respond accordingly. We are invited to surrender and to be of service.

This is huge, and the shift is difficult. Almost all of the systems created by humanity, the systems shaping our everyday lives, are based on organizational systems that depend on individuals gaining power in order to be called leaders. Whether in government, business, finance, education, health, politics, religion, arts, or sports, these leaders are expected to predict where a system should be going and then control conditions so that everything remains geared toward the predicted outcome.

In the past decade I have had hundreds of conversations in which I experienced resistance and pushback against the story of self-organization, be it in theory or in practice. There are predictable, core concerns which arise again and again—the causes of the resistance. It feels essential to explore these concerns deeply, to understand and transcend what holds us back from stepping into the potential of this still widely uncharted territory of self-organization.

3

Understanding What is Holding Us Back

Seeing the patterns that hold people back from the journey into new self-organized ways of working brought me right back to my own past experience, and a time when I suffered a severe burn out. For months during this personal crisis, I was more or less tied to home, overwhelmed by almost everything. For most of a year, it was impossible for me to do any work.

A serious personal financial upheaval and a divorce preceded this experience, leaving me a single mother of my then 9-year-old son, in the middle of redefining my work as an entrepreneur and independent consultant and coach, with no money. I entered into a healing process through which I dealt with all of the obvious things that had been draining my energy to the point of complete breakdown. I saw aspects of my life that had been causing harm and changed many things including the way I went about my work. My self-understanding was growing but remained somewhat superficial during this time of breakdown and recovery.

Years later, when I started to see patterns of resistance and push back in others through my professional work, I was able to recognize some of the internal dynamics I'd lived through during my own personal crisis. I suddenly understood that a big contributor to my burn out had been my internal struggles—searching to understand my personal purpose and encountering resistance within my existing belief system to fully seeing and embodying my purpose because it could potentially require me to change things and let go of so much.

Today I am deeply grateful for my past experience, as it enables me to hold huge empathy and compassion for people who are on the same journey. The shift into self-organization requires *more* than a shift into structures of distributed authority and decision making, of autonomy and empowerment, of liberated structures and conscious communications, of presence and mindfulness, of wholeness, of purpose and self-management, of shifting power, and more. It is all of this—which you can explore in numerous great books, articles, presentations, videos and podcasts—and so much more, and beyond what we yet know.

This shift cannot be seen simply as "something we do in our organizations". It is part of a much greater shift, one that concerns human consciousness as a whole. It is a shift that concerns all aspects of our life. We cannot change our mindset regarding this new way in which we do work together without changing the way we relate to ourselves, to one another, to the world, and to life in general.

These realizations brought with them a total turmoil of emotions, including feelings of overwhelm and helplessness. It was all too big. Was I facing a need to save the world as a whole? And if so, who was I to do that? I felt stuck, and the work that I had been doing with joy and passion suddenly felt fragmented, or even useless. I had this sense—again—that something important was missing. But what?

Again, it was my JournaLogue practice, in combination with an embodiment practice that I had learned over many years from the wonderful Arawana Hayashi (see textbox), which helped me move out of my stuck state. It led me to open up towards the contributions of wonderful people who were telling new stories, bringing new narratives into the world that seemed so aligned with the stories I had learned to embrace. I was able to access a feeling of companionship for the journey, recognize I was not alone, and continue my quest with—using Theory U terminology—an open mind, open heart, and open will.

> *Social Presencing Theater—The Art of Making a True Move*, as described on Arawana Hayashi's Website:
>
> "Social Presencing Theater (SPT) is a social technology developed to enable, and facilitate systems change. It has been developed through a collaboration of MIT Professor Otto Scharmer, and Arawana Hayashi, as a part of the Presencing Institute.
>
> SPT is one arm of the Presencing Institute. It is an emerging art form that explores the creative potential of Theory U and presencing. The word theater comes from the Greek *thea*, which means "the act of seeing." The word, theater, can be defined as a "place of enactment of significant events or actions." SPT emerges from the community to enable that community to collectively see itself and enact its emerging future."

The first step I took then was to take a fresh look at my personal purpose. For some years I had expressed my guiding purpose as, "the manifestation of love in the way we do our work in the world, both individually and collectively."

While this still sounded true to me, through my purpose quest I found something that had been missing. A new definition of my purpose emerged: "The unification of love and power."

After overcoming the first wave of overwhelm that this purpose definition created, it all began to make sense. Viewed through this lens, everything in my life reoriented towards this purpose. I could clearly see what would help me move forward with my work in the world.

Focusing on the manifestation of love had made much of my work so inspiring, however all the love I could access and convey still didn't help me resolve the resistance I had encountered, both within myself and within others. The realization that this resistance was related to power gave me new insight and clarity. Stories about love and power are deeply ingrained in the belief system of humanity, and I knew that—along with the shift in consciousness—these stories would eventually transcend as well.

My purpose helped me through the overwhelm of the "save the world" energy, as it gave me an orientation to bring into the world what wanted to come through me. It was about creating tangible, accessible, and approachable ways to integrate the unification of love and power into our everyday lives, no matter how small the steps. I began to believe that through this purpose orientation I could make a contribution, be of service to the greater whole, and bring my unique gifts to the world just as every single human being on this planet can. No more, no less.

To understand more about the roots of the pain experienced by so many confronted with the shift in organizing required two things:

1. Zooming out, or seeking to understand the bigger systemic picture, helped me be clearer about my story of self-organization as a way forward for us humans to collectively serve people and planet at the same time.

2. Zooming back in, with a focus shifted away from new forms of organizing to the *personal* journey that this shift triggers.

Like a pendulum, my perspective now swings between a zoomed out, global view and a zoomed in, personal view to help me clearly see my work in the larger context.

Zooming out

When zooming out to look at the bigger picture, one can see a consciousness shift for humanity rooted in the understanding of the connectedness of everything. Many writers and thinkers are exploring the infinite interdependence of everything. Understanding and integrating this will enable us to fully step into new ways of being together, not only in the way we organize our endeavors, but in all aspects of our lives: with our loved ones, with our communities, with our bioregions, with humanity at large, and with everything that is our livelihood.

To organize our human endeavors with a focus on purpose is a vital aspect of new ways of being and becoming, nourishing both people and planet. This is the most powerful way for humanity to bring into being what is truly needed by the greater whole as well as by its parts. It is what nature has been doing since the beginning of time as it has self-organized its evolution.

We humans were tuned into the rhythm of nature until not too long ago in our species' history. Our primordial way of being was connected and interdependent. At some point of its evolution, an ever-growing part of humanity began to lose its sense of being an interconnected part of the web of life. Many believe that the change occurred when we moved into the agricultural age, but—after reading David Graeber's and David Wengrow's book *The Dawn of Everything*—it doesn't seem to be so simple. In whatever way it evolved, humanity today widely has developed a fallacious belief that our species has the power to control practically everything.

With the seed of disconnection sown, we eventually forgot that we are, individually and collectively, interdependent parts of everything. Mental constructs around power let us think up and define outputs that we then claim are, and believe to be, the desirable and necessary future states.

We know that our capacity to predict and control outcomes has brought tremendous development, education, health, and prosperity to humanity over the past centuries. We are starting to understand the amount of destruction it has brought as well.

Climate consequences, social and racial injustice, genocides, and the widening gap between rich and poor are outputs of the systems we've designed, to name only the most obvious. All the good things humanity has brought upon itself, and even our survival as a whole, are now under threat because of our ignorance of the shadow side of what we have been calling progress.

The threats presented by these shadows are real, they are here, and they are urgent. There's a new phenomenon at play for humanity, too—due to advances in technology, all the issues that threaten our livelihood are global. It is the first time in the history of our species that the threats that we face cannot be solved on a local level. It seems that seeing the connectedness of everything will be vital for humanity's survival.

Zooming back in

For years, a large part of what I offered through my work had been triggering resistance through inviting my clients to challenge their own belief systems and examine their underlying stories. Drawing from my own journey and personal experience and from what I had seen in others, I developed a framework called "Language of Spaces". With the processes of this framework, I was inviting people into introspection and detailed perspective taking, a foundational capacity to be able to fully embrace self-organization and the new way of being with ourselves and with others. Almost everybody I took through the foundational process of Language of Spaces for the first time said the same words: "wow, this isn't easy, but it is so powerful!" Until fairly recently—and despite the apparent power of this approach—almost no one came back to continue working with this approach.

Researching why this might be the case, I began to see patterns: what it was, in general, that was creating so much resistance and holding so many of us back from stepping deeper into new ways of (inter)being.

I found that the patterns of resistance were triggered by both fear and overwhelm.

Fear

Fear can be anything from extremely useful to extremely limiting. Without going deeper into psychology and neuroscience, we can roughly define fear as an emotional and physiological reaction to something our brain categorizes as a threat. This can be anything from a threat to our life or the threat of not getting our core needs met, to something small like the threat of bumping into someone or the threat of being late for a dinner invitation.

It is amazing how *few* innate fears we humans have. Most of our fears are acquired through our socialization and are therefore based in the stories we have learned to believe are true about our world and the life we are living.

Depending on the level of fear we are feeling, our brain shifts partially or fully toward ways of avoiding the threat. The resulting behaviors can be placed on a wide continuum, ranging from a full-scale "flight, fight, or freeze" response to calmly deciding against something and walking away from it. To focus on avoiding the threat, and depending on the level and intensity of fear we are feeling, our brain may shut out some of its parts . . . especially the parts related to more rational, complex thought. This means that when our behavior is driven by fear, we are acting with limited brain capacity.

In my work with clients moving through the transition to New Work, the resistance I was seeing was almost always based in the fear of not getting core needs met. Of course, we are all different and have a large variety of needs and desires, but ultimately human needs can be subsumed under three main categories. We are driven by the need for

1. acceptance,
2. independence, and
3. security.

While all of us probably have needs in each of those categories, most of us tend to prioritize one of them. While everything around us seems to change and we are faced with unknowns about where this journey is taking us, we may become preoccupied with being accepted, keeping our independence, or staying safe.

Being accepted, being independent, and being safe can mean something entirely different for each of us, but one thing remains the same: when we are faced with changes and we don't know where the change is taking us, we can experience fear. Being wired as we are, this experience of fear - as mentioned before - shuts down parts of our brains and leads to behaviors based on this limitation.

Overwhelm

The rational perspective on overwhelm is, "I have too much on my plate—I am overwhelmed by it all." The psychological and neurological foundations of the feeling of overwhelm are highly complex and, as is widely known, are often at the root of the increasing phenomena of burnout and depression. Thankfully, many psychiatrists, therapists, coaches, and others in health-oriented professions are highly skilled to help us deal with the negative consequences of overwhelm.

Temporary overwhelm results from simply having too many tasks that need to be attended to at the same time, and/or done under time pressure or lack of other resources, such as financials or knowledge and skill. The overwhelm comes when we feel that we won't be able to do it all, but continue to try and make it work nonetheless. The positive side of this kind of overwhelm is that it draws our attention towards the need to change or improve something. This is where tools for time- and self-management and personal productivity can be extremely helpful.

There is another form of overwhelm, which is not a temporary phenomenon but something deeper, more existential, and more constantly threatening. Its roots reach into our shadows. It is the form of overwhelm that can make us sick, because instead of reducing what we have on our plate, we tend to try even harder to deal with everything in a way that we feel is necessary. The level of stress increases and we don't allow ourselves the brakes our body and mind need to regain energy and strength. It is our belief system that keeps us in this rat race

The boundaries between these two forms of overwhelm are blurred, and it can be hard to recognize when we are moving into dangerous terrain. It has become "normal", or almost expected in our society, that we are constantly busy, busy, busy. At the same time, we are constantly distracted by ongoing demand for being available through technology.

In my work with my clients, I've encountered the whole spectrum of overwhelm. While coaching clients to explore their inner conditions that led to overwhelm, I also looked to understand the outside causes. I saw a pattern that helped me understand the complexity of the journey into self-organization even better. I recognized three different fields of awareness that play together and cause this more existential crisis of overwhelm.

1. We are increasingly aware of the global issues humanity is facing. As mentioned before, we are universally faced with the climate crisis, social and racial injustice, war, genocide, widening economic disparity, and other profoundly harmful issues, and most of us realize that impactful action is needed.

2. The conventional way of doing business is a) contributing to these large-scale global issues and b) making people miserable and sick. Whether from the inside of a company or from the outside as a coach, consultant, facilitator, or teacher, people want to contribute to making the workplace better for both people and planet.

3. With the combination of the world's needs and our systems' exacerbations of the crises, the need for a radical shift in the way we do our work in the world is increasingly clear. This brings many of us to questioning our personal patterns and belief systems, which makes it clear that this journey begins within ourselves.

Does any of this ring true to you?

Identifying these three fields of awareness, I suddenly realized that these combined factors had been the source of my own overwhelm. For me, the overwhelm stemmed from feeling helpless while wanting to save the world. These three points—the world's need, the harm of current systems, and our necessity to make a radical shift—are inseparably connected. If we engage with one, the other two are there with it, no matter what.

A few examples

From purposeful work to personal development: let's say you are engaged in a movement, network, or company that focuses on a specific social justice issue (point 1). Since the conventional power hierarchy has injustice baked into it, you see that a different way of doing work together is needed if you are to be effective. This new form of organizing must use just methods to address justice issues (point 2). Finding a different way of working together requires letting go of the many beliefs we have all been programmed with through our upbringing and socialization. You and your colleagues struggle with, and need to learn about, your beliefs and patterns around leadership and power. Only by exploring, individually and collectively, how you can shift the stories that you have been telling yourself for so long can you effectively adopt a way of working that is values-aligned with your social justice work. This leads you into a personal development journey (point 3).

From personal growth to greater awareness: perhaps your life has brought you to the point where you are consciously attempting to understand yourself and others better. You are working to see your shadows and deepen your spirituality (point 3). Your work context begins to feel uncomfortable in two ways. For one, you see how you and others are trapped in a system that limits expression of your full potential and creates dependency (point 2). For another, you begin to see the many ways that the profit motivation of business is contributing to crises in climate, social justice, and economic justice (point 1).

From a change at work to a change within: Perhaps your work environment is shifting into any one of the various organizational practices broadly known as Next Stage Organizing due to a decision made somewhere in the power hierarchy (point 2). The organization shifts from a profit-driven to a purpose-driven orientation, which creates a collective sense of serving the greater whole (point 1). In the beginning you feel excited and motivated, but the change soon triggers questions about what this can mean for you. As you explore these questions, you begin to learn that the outside shift and the inside shift are deeply connected. You understand that your new way of working won't be sustainable or tolerable without an inner journey (point 3).

Whether you begin shifting at the point of the world's challenges, your organization's operations, or your inner life, the shift will always connect you to the other two realms. Whether consciously or unconsciously, we are faced with three questions at the same time:

1. How can I contribute to positive change in a world fraught with challenges?

2. How can I help shift the way we humans collectively do our work in the world, so that people and planet are both served?

3. How can I empower myself to contribute through embodying my personal purpose?

Depending on the current conditions in your life, you may tend to prioritize one of these questions over the others. They nevertheless remain inseparable, whether you are conscious of it or not. Every single one is big, and in itself can easily leave you with a feeling of overwhelm and/or fear.

Facing fear and overwhelm

One way or the other, we all live with feelings of fear and overwhelm. It's healthy to have a number of strategies to deal with these emotions. When we are aware of our fears and overwhelm and are willing to face them, we can find healthy ways forward, learn about ourselves, and integrate our emotions into our thoughts and actions in a constructive way.

When we are not aware that our behaviors are guided by fear and/or overwhelm, which happens fairly often, we come to resistance. This is something we often see in those challenged by the shift in consciousness necessitated by the journey into self-organization.

At this point we need to be clear on what we mean by "resistance" in the context of this book. For our purposes, we can subsume under the term "resistance" all behavior patterns that people use, consciously and subconsciously, to avoid the inevitable learning journey and mind shift that occur on the path to self-organization. These behavior patterns are generally geared towards avoiding the triggers of fear and overwhelm, which is a natural way for humans to react. There are usually very good reasons for avoiding the challenges of the ongoing consciousness shift—reasons which often show that someone is either not yet at the point to question and change their belief system and embrace the ongoing consciousness shift, or that they are already on that journey, but feel stuck.

To generalize, one doesn't start a journey of change and evolution without experiencing a calling—a longing, or a sense that something is amiss and isn't serving any more. At first, one might resist accepting that it is time to move on. One might even begin to explore new possibilities without full awareness that that's what's going on. Before long, however, one will come face to face with the fact that it is time to grow.

Once on this journey, there is no good or bad—there is only the varying terrain that presents itself to us, how we experience it, and what we decide to do to navigate it. On this journey, we are likely to encounter familiar companions—challenges and behaviors of resistance that show up during times of uncertainty, and that hold lessons for us if we are able to spend time learning from them.

Systemic change into the paradigm of the new world of work tends to trigger these behaviors of resistance. In my experience, they tend to fall into three general categories. Each holds information about old cultural stories and patterns that can be unlearned, liberating us to learn new stories and new ways of being.

Rationalizing

Every belief system has a valid rationale behind it. All our beliefs are based on experiences and have at some time proven to be useful to us. Based on this usefulness, we decide to believe they are "true". Even dysfunctional coping mechanisms are usually rooted in a time, earlier in life, when the mechanism kept us safe. When we are challenged in our beliefs and not (yet) ready to question them, one way we react is to emphasize the many good reasons why this belief is good and right, while the other (seen as contradictory) belief is bad and wrong.

Here are some examples of the rationale we hear as reactions to the ongoing global shift towards self-organization:

"It's a fact—some people are more powerful than others."

"People are either leaders or followers."

"Many people don't want to be responsible—they want to be told what to do."

"Without managers in charge to control what is going on, everything breaks down in chaos."

"Ultimately, someone has to be responsible".

"Look at how successful the management hierarchy has been— at the progress and prosperity it has brought to humanity."

"Look at the animal world. Every pack has a leader."

Each of these statements can be considered true, and also not. As always, we can say, "it depends—on context and perspective".

Resistance is usually present when statements like these are used to argue that something is right and/or a truth, and to prove that a controversial statement is wrong and/or untrue. When we get caught up in this kind of discussion, we are drawn into an inner process of finding the best argument to prove our perspective. In order to do that, we draw from what we already know, and put things together so that they make sense based on our rational—hence the term "rationalizing". For this process we mainly use the part of the brain that is in charge of rational thinking and logic. This diminishes access to other parts of our experience, including feeling and connecting.

Withdrawing

People with a tendency toward this behavior strategy engage less and less over time, withdrawing themselves from active participation in anything that has to do with shifting into a new way of working together. When asked how they are, they often answer, "fine," even when they are not. They try to do their work as best they can while staying under the radar.

Some people are sure that what is going on in their company is just this season's "change management" thing, and that it will pass. Some people get sick, which sometimes leads to long term absences caused by depression and burnout. I know from my own experience with serious burnout that it can be caused in part by our withdrawal from life and work—even from people who care about us and might have the willingness to help.

When we have a sense of what we would like to do to embody our personal purpose, but don't have the courage to talk about it or do anything about it, we exhibit another form of withdrawal. Limiting beliefs regarding our core needs (acceptance, security, independence) underpin this behavior.

Hyperactivity

For some of us, our *modus operandi* when we feel threatened is to get very busy, to work very hard, to start many projects at the same time, and to work really long hours. Through Language of Spaces sessions, I've seen clients reveal many reasons for these behaviors. Some feel confusion about what is going on and turn to hyperactivity to a) hide their confusion, and b) demonstrate their willingness. Others fear losing the status and privilege of a manager, a position which they may have worked hard to attain. Hyperactive behavior can sometimes even appear to be aggressive, while it is actually a defense mechanism to protect against perceived loss of acceptance, security, or independence.

These resistant behaviors show up when people are not yet ready to question their belief systems, because letting go—even a little bit—feels like a risk. If we change our beliefs, we change as a person. Questions arise, often subconsciously: when I change, will I still be accepted and loved? Will I still be independent? Will I still be safe? As long as we are not sure that we will get our core needs met, we will resist change. From our individual perspective, this is a very wise survival strategy—until it causes us to ignore our calling or fall into stagnation.

Hearing the call

Everywhere in the world, people are hearing a call to change and longing for a different life. A life with meaning, with more ease and simplicity, with less hassle and pressure, with more calm and joy, and with stronger connection to the really important things of life. They are yearning to better understand their unique gift to the world—their personal purpose—and how to embody it. These yearnings show up in people from all walks of life. Entrepreneurs, CEOs, employees at all hierarchical levels of companies of all sizes, consultants, coaches, independent service providers, and many on the journey into self-organization, located on all continents, are hearing the call.

There is a global community coming together around this movement, and it is growing. If you are reading this book, you are probably part of it. This global shift is significant enough that we might assume humanity as a whole is on the threshold of a consciousness shift, of which self-organization is an important part.

The call is clear, yes—and yet hearing the call and heeding it are two different matters entirely. In the human process of Individuation, resisting the call is a very real, common, and sometimes painful experience.

Humanity has already created an abundance of beautiful teachings and practices for all aspects of our being—body, mind, heart, and spirit. They support us in our personal Individuation processes as well as to grow collectively in different groups, such as in our families, tribes, companies, and communities. Nonetheless, it's clear that many in the New World of Work are still experiencing resistance, and limited by pain, fear, and overwhelm. In addition to the wonderful resources and ways that are already available to us, I began to wonder what else could support this global community—a community with as much diversity as humanity itself—to continue on its journey. What are the shared aspects of our struggles on this path toward more collective fulfillment and impact, and how can we resource ourselves and one another to continue forward with more freedom and joy?

From my many conversations and experiences with so many inspiring people all over the world, I began to see a global community taking form, and to see four stories that this community appeared to share. At the core of each of these stories is something that connects the global community and drives our shared quest for meaning. I set out to increase awareness of these four stories, show how they are connected, and through that nourish the conditions for global collective learning and expansion of consciousness.

4
Four Shared Stories of the Global Community

The story of stories

I was raised in Austria, in what I would call a conservative environment. In my family, the world was defined by what is good or bad, right or wrong, true or untrue. *Good* was defined mostly in the context of behavior. To give an example, table-manners were a really important issue, and of course "our" table manners were the good ones. A neighbor who didn't know how to hold a knife, or how to position his hands while eating, or how to keep his mouth shut when chewing, had bad manners. Though the conclusion was never explicitly spoken out, bad table manners indicated that someone was somehow not "good" in a general sense. This was such an implicit story, but for me as a child it was taken for granted as truth.

I was the youngest of six children. That was already a bit unusual. Add to it the fact that we were all girls, and our family seemed quite out of the norm. Saying that I was one of six sisters always brought a distinct response. I cannot tell you how often in my life I have heard one of these two reactions: "the wish for the son is the father of many daughters!" (mostly followed by laughter), or "the poor father!" Do you hear the stories?

I was almost thirty by the time I was able to begin to change some of the deeply engraved stories of my childhood—to begin the journey of getting to know myself beyond those limitations. It shook my world to learn about constructivism, and how we form our mental map and our unique reality of the world. It took me a long time to digest what this meant, but once I did, a whole new world opened up for me to explore.

C.G. Jung said, "life really does begin at forty. Up until then, you are just doing research". This quote makes me laugh in that it reminds me so much of myself. Today I would say that the research never really ends, it just takes on a different quality as more meaningful stories begin to enrich one's life.

When we hear the word story, we often think of a fairy tale, a fiction book, a legend, a theatrical play, or a movie. We see *story* as the expression of a fiction, in any one of these forms.

Stories play a much bigger role in our life—to a degree far beyond what many of us have in our awareness. Stories shape our reality. They form what we believe about ourselves and about the world around us.

The historian Yuval Noah Harari is one contemporary author and speaker who manages to vividly tell the story of stories. In his book "Sapiens - A Brief History of Humankind", he says: "there are no gods in the universe, no nations, no money, no human rights, no laws, and no justice outside the common imagination of human beings. None of these things exists outside the stories that people invent and tell one another."

He and many others have written about why stories and storytelling are indispensable for the survival of humanity. When it comes to stories, every human being, no matter where on the globe, lives by stories. It is a pattern that is applied by every single human on this planet.

Our belief system consists of stories—those we grew up with and were socialized with. From the patterns of the collective unconscious—the Archetypes—to the patterns that are specific to our families, our communities, and our cultures, stories shape how we see the world and ourselves in it. They give us orientation and a sense of belonging with those who tell themselves the same or similar stories. We learn from hearing new stories, though we also resist learning from new or unfamiliar stories when they appear to be incompatible with the ones we already believe.

Based on our stories, we tend to categorize: right or wrong, true or untrue. We tend to place our categorization anywhere on the continuum between those polarities. The more important a story feels to us, the more we tend to go to the extremes of those polarities. When we collectively categorize something as true, we form communities around this truth with a sense of shared meaning. Social creatures that we are, we can not survive without a sense of belonging, and this sense is based in shared stories.

Another term for "story" might be "cultural metaphor." Aboriginal Australian author Tyson Yunkaporta also writes on the power of cultural metaphors in *Sand Talk*. Writing on the subject of our obligations and relationships, our roles and relationships with creation—he says, "the way we work with this knowledge is by positioning, sharing, and adapting our cultural metaphors."

The power of story to shape behavior and outcomes cannot be overstated. As an example, as we face a sixth great extinction and accelerating climate consequences, we can look at ecological imbalances as direct outcomes of our cultural metaphors. Author Jeremy Lent points out this connection in his book *The Patterning Instinct* as he addresses how our metaphors shape our worldviews and actions. "By prizing reason over emotion, splitting human existence into mind and body, and then defining humanity only by its mind, we set the cognitive foundations for the scientific and industrial revolutions that transformed the world. In our relationship to the external world, we pursued a similar path of disconnection, finding meaning in transcendence while desacralizing the earth, creating root metaphors of nature as an enemy to be conquered and a machine to be engineered."

When gathering around shared stories and meaning that are categorized as truths, collectives can feel called to act. This can be a beautiful initiative to help people in despair—for example, mobilizing to help refugees. It can also be an incredible atrocity, such as in the commission of war and genocide. All of these collective actions are based on stories that we tell ourselves and that we believe are true.

> Additional Resources on the Power of Stories:
>
> Brian Boyd: *On the Origin of Stories: Evolution, Cognition, and Fiction*; Belknap Press: An Imprint of Harvard University Press; Reprint edition (November 15, 2010)
>
> Martin Puchner: *The Written World: The Power of Stories to Shape People, History, and Civilizations*; Random House; 1st edition (October 24, 2017)
>
> *Our fiction addiction: Why humans need stories* https://www.bbc.com/culture/article/20180503-our-fiction-addiction-why-humans-need-stories
>
> *How Telling Stories Makes Us Human:* https://time.com/5043166/storytelling-evolution/

Communities form around shared stories. With the meta-pattern of storytelling shaping so much collective human behavior, we can zoom in and ask, "what are the key shared stories that connect and empower those around the globe who seek lives filled with more meaning?"

The story of purpose

Today the term "purpose" is one of many buzzwords in the business world, in the fields of personal development, happiness, and wellbeing, and in spiritual teachings.

In my early professional days, the word was neither prominent in the business nor personal growth contexts. It had no relevance for my professional and personal paths—at least not consciously. Looking back, I can see how my life was always driven by purpose (as I believe everyone's life is), but I wasn't consciously aware of it. I can now see that I was battling to favor my rational decision-making over the intuition coming from a place inside of me that I had not yet discovered. It was a battle grounded in separation—in not being connected to my source, my soul, my Inner Wisdom.

I know now that it takes a lot of energy to try to fight and shut down the voice of intuition in favor of rationalizing. For me, this battle led to severe burnout.

My first explicit expression of my personal purpose was, "the manifestation of love in the way we do our work in the world." This definition didn't emerge from consciously exploring my purpose but emerged following a time when I had over and over again asked myself the questions, "what is really important to me?" and "what do I really want to do?".

At the time, my full-time work as a systemic business consultant and coach financially supported my life as a single mother. While I had already realized that something felt off or was missing, and had begun to search for alternatives, I was troubled by inner voices going round and round in my head.

"What does 'the manifestation of love' even mean?", "do you really think anybody is going to pay you for that?", "you'll never be able to make a living from bringing love into the business world!", "nobody is going to take you seriously!" These doubts made it hard for me to follow the guidance of my inner wisdom into greater purpose alignment.

Two opposing things were very real to me at the time: the sense of excitement and inspiration I felt when thinking about engaging in the manifestation of love in the business world, and the fear that I would seriously risk my source of income. Much later I learned that one of my biggest shadows is a recurring pattern of self-sabotage. I was holding a general belief that I didn't deserve to follow my dreams. My doubts and concerns, which were the voices of this shadow, won out over the inspiration. I decided to stay with what I was doing, even if it didn't feel right anymore. It was the safe way to go.

While staying on the "safe" path and continuing with my business as usual, I didn't quite give up on my inspiration. I continued to learn and get trained—in Holacracy, at that time—and began to deliver workshops about this different way of doing work in service to purpose. With my growing understanding of the role of purpose in new ways of working, I strove after a deeper understanding of its meaning. I did all that in addition to my "real work". Later I realized that at the time I felt profoundly divided—as though I were living in two separate universes.

I was completely unaware of the battle going on inside of me - my purpose trying to talk to me, and my shadow getting in the way. I fully tuned into a "when/then" pattern: when I have built enough interest in this new way of working and am making money with it, then I can stop doing the work that I don't actually want to do any more.

Going through a divorce, adapting to parenting as a single mother, and adding this level of complexity to my work life, it was only a matter of time until something would change—I would either be willing to see, or be forced to see, the profound harm of this divided existence. I didn't give up easily but in the end my body took over and I collapsed.

While my burnout was profoundly painful, I am now grateful for the experience. I can say, as can so many who've gone through something similar, that it triggered the biggest and most meaningful transition phase in my life. It opened me up to a whole new level of consciousness, and consequently to the decision that my purpose will guide not only my work in the world, but my entire life.

My burnout and recovery helped me understand that we—all of us—are here for a reason. Every one of us has a gift to bring, and life is about finding out what that gift is and how to embody and manifest it. There are probably as many ways of doing that as there are humans on this planet and it is for each of us to find our unique way. This is part of the beauty of it all.

As I recovered and found a new path forward, guided by my purpose, I engaged wholeheartedly with what I felt as a calling: understanding self-organization and how it could serve people and planet equally. This led me to continue developing and offering the framework of "Language of Spaces", co-founding encode.org llc and Evolution at Work LLC, and engaging in the development of the For-Purpose Enterprise and the Symbiotic Enterprise.

At first, doing this work felt like a homecoming—yet, somewhere along the way, I noticed something missing in the way my purpose was defined. At a gathering of encode.org, in what we call a "Purpose Agent Meetup", we explored both individual and organizational purposes. Tim Kelley, founder of the True Purpose Institute and author of the book *True Purpose*, supported this process.

The beauty of this experience is hard to describe. When the expression of one's personal purpose shifts, it is not as if it is wholly different. It is as if it expands, gains focus, and gains depth. It becomes illuminated. Suddenly, one sees more and can be guided with greater clarity in all the actions that follow. At the same time, one always knows there's more to come, and not yet seen. There is a journey to travel before more can reveal itself to you—the exploration of embodiment and manifestation of purpose.

It was a privilege to be facilitated by Tim through the process of gaining more clarity about my purpose. Its expression shifted. From "the manifestation of love in the way we do our work in the world" it changed to "the unification of love and power", and I will say more about this shift later in the book.

The journey of exploring, embodying, and manifesting purpose for me was and is both beautiful and challenging on so many levels. It has a quality of meaning and authenticity that helps me face challenges, working through and learning from them. My belief is that this journey will continue until the day I leave this life and move on. It is the journey of exploring, embodying, and manifesting my soul potential. It is the journey of becoming ever more of who I truly am and of fulfilling the reason why I am here. Each and every one of us is on this path, knowingly or otherwise.

While living into this new consciousness around my purpose, and through many conversations, I realized that the word purpose carries different meanings for different people. My perspectives, and my meaning making, are both profound and limited, in that they can never be anything more or less than *mine*. Somewhere along my journey I let go of the concepts of "what is right" and "what is wrong". While there is no universal truth, there is the possibility—through sharing about our lived experiences and our perspectives—to arrive at shared understanding and mutual growth.

This connects back to the meta-story of stories. When I share how I see something, or share my perspective, it is the story as it has formed up for me over the course of my life. To me this story sounds true at this moment. I have no expectation for my story to be seen as the truth. The beauty of the concept of "story" is that telling it feels like stretching out my hands towards others and offering something. It is totally up to the others if they like it, and if they want to take it—as a whole, in select parts, or not at all.

For me the intention of telling my story is to create resonance; resonance with the field of stories others tell as well. Resonance with your story. I hope my story adds to your and others' stories, and I hope you and many others will offer your story. When that happens, it will add to and enrich mine. This resonance is what enables a story to spread and travel—even around the entire globe.

So here is my story, rooted in my current understanding about systemic purpose, personal purpose, and my conviction that being guided by purpose is vitally important to humanity.

Systemic purpose

My first conscious encounter with "purpose" was about a company's purpose. I learned to understand why purpose is so important.

You may have heard the sentence "purpose is the new boss." This concept, of course, only works for companies that have actually shifted to being purpose-guided, where an organizational system actually has no bosses anymore. It means that every decision made and every action taken while doing the company's work must answer the question, "how does this serve the purpose of the company?". Absent a boss to tell you what to do and to evaluate whether you "did a good job", service to purpose becomes the measure of success.

In exploring corporate purpose, questions about the originating source of a company's purpose came up. At the time, I found scarce resources on this topic—they mostly consisted of Simon Sinek's *Start With WHY* and Tim Kelley's *True Purpose*. Both books are wonderful, and very inspirational. Still, I am thankful that over the years this has become a very rich field with many great books, articles, and speeches. When combining all I could find with my own personal experience, here's how I describe a company's purpose.

A company is a system. Just like any other system—institution, community, movement, city, society, or ecosystem—it has its purpose. When a need arises from within such a system and one or more people feel called to engage and do something to fulfill this need, activities to organize that work will begin and a new system will form to serve this need. This is why I call it "systemic purpose".

The new system can be anything from a temporary initiative to a network, a movement, a company, or something else. The need around which it forms can arise from global causes such as the climate crisis or racism, or from local issues like homelessness in winter or food delivery opportunities.

"Purpose" is a value-free term. Performing any coordinated activity guided by serving a specific need is "serving a purpose", no matter where the need comes from and what it is. Allowing myself to see this, and even to speak it out, was a major challenge for a very long time. Many of us have been involved in conversations about how the purpose of business is ultimately about making money, or about how a company producing weapons is bad.

I have allowed myself to be sucked into these energy-consuming and tiring discussions countless times, and they have always left me with a sense of desperation. It wasn't until I could understand purpose on the same level as my understanding of the connectedness of everything that I could let go of trying to fight what I believed to be a "bad" or "harmful" purpose.

A company organizes its work around any one (or more) need. The "why" is to serve the need(s). As systems change in an evolutionary manner, so do their needs. This then informs the evolution of a company's purpose, which makes a company's purpose an evolutionary phenomenon as well—it changes over time.

Seen from this perspective, a company forms around its purpose because people in general have a basic desire to be of service. When connecting this to the story of the interconnectedness and interdependence of everything, serving the needs of a system always means serving a part of the greater whole. This means **a purpose-guided company serves the greater whole through serving its parts**.

This perspective touched me to the core. This was what I wanted to fully engage with: to find ways to share this story, the story of how we humans can organize in such a way that the entire company (a system in itself) always strives to serve the greater whole.

What was it that touched me so deeply and fueled my passion for this work? This question brought me back to my personal purpose. I was aware that the defined purpose of each company I was engaged with was very inspiring and showed me why it was worth engaging for. Each resonated with my personal purpose, but none were *the same as* my personal purpose.

Personal purpose

It is so important to be aware of our own personal purpose. This enables us to make conscious decisions guided by purpose, which means all our decisions can be aligned and help us embody and manifest our purpose in all aspects of our life.

When it comes to making decisions about where we invest our time, talent, and energy to do our work in the world, there are two helpful questions. We can ask ourselves:

1. Do I want to serve this (company's) purpose, seeing how it is much bigger than myself?
2. Will this work also contribute to me embodying and manifesting my personal purpose?

If your answer to both these questions is "yes", what you feel is *purpose alignment*. You will be inspired and passionate about what you are doing.

On a deeper level, what really is personal purpose? Saying that it is the "why" that I am here for didn't satisfy my curiosity. I needed to explore further. How does that "why" define itself? Where is its source?

The answers to these questions can be found, in part, through learnings in three different areas: our personal development, our soul, and our states of awareness.

Personal development

Many interesting models describe personal development. Each, when studied, brings new perspectives and insights. Great thought leaders, including Sigmund Freud, Carl Jung, Erik Erikson, Jean Piaget, Lawrence Kohlberg, Jean Gebser, Jane Loevinger, Clare W. Graves, Don Beck, Ken Wilber, Susanne Cook-Greuter, Robert Kegan, Terri O'Fallon, and many more have brought incredible richness of knowledge and inspiration into the field. Every time I learn about a perspective on human development, I learn something new, specifically about social dynamics and about myself and my life.

Taking a more general approach, I can see a pattern in almost every model which is sufficient to explain how studying personal development helped me understand what personal purpose is and how we can connect to it.

Phases of development

In a general sense, we can describe our personal development journey in three phases:

> **Phase 1:** As a newborn baby, we don't yet experience ourselves as an individual. We are fused, generally with our mother and with the little of the world around us of which we are aware. Our primary need is the sense of being loved and cared for. We are not aware of the boundary between "I" and "you", "they", or "it".
>
> **Phase 2:** At some point we discover ourselves as "I", gaining a sense of self separate from "other", and we begin to form our individual identity. We need a sense of "who am I", different from "you", with the possibility to form a healthy ego, or a healthy sense of self. We need to find our own place in the world.
>
> **Phase 3:** With a healthy ego and sense of self, we can turn to explore outside our ego—we understand ourselves better as we learn that there is more to us than our ego. We need a sense of who we truly are in the greater scheme of things, and experience curiosity around the deeper meaning of life.

This third phase shows up in many forms for different people, and is generally guided by questions around why we are here, what is really important to us, and what mark or footprint we want to leave behind once we move on from our life in this world. We yearn to understand the deeper meaning of our life and our purpose.

Soul

This yearning for a deeper understanding of my personal purpose led me into a whole new depth of introspection. I went through a number of different practices to support my quest, and the more I allowed myself to open up to this journey, the more I developed a feeling that I was connecting to my essence—my soul. I began to understand my soul as the source of my purpose. Driven by curiosity, as I always am, I wanted to understand. What is "soul"? How does one grow one's awareness of it?

Almost all philosophical, religious, and spiritual teachings speak about *soul* in one way or another. While finding great inspiration in many of those different perspectives and their similarities and differences, I had great difficulty in finding words to express the story that had begun to form up inside of me. Words can create some form of boundary through meaning making, implying that something means "this", not "that".

The writings and teachings of Rupert Spira[9] and Bill Plotkin[10] helped me find the words to express the perspective that had formed inside of me.

> *"Soul is your true space/sphere/location within consciousness*
> *and expresses itself on all levels of being."*
> –Rupert Spira

> *"Your soul is your true nature, your true place in nature.*
> *Each of us is born with a treasure, an essence, a seed of quiescent potential, secreted for safekeeping in the center of our being. Our personal destiny is to become that treasure through our actions."*
> –Bill Plotkin

In order to grasp the concept of soul, I found I needed to understand something even bigger than soul: the realm of everything, or *the infinite realm of all being and becoming.*

---

[9] Rupert Spira: Presence, Volume I: The Art of Peace and Happiness; Volume II: The Intimacy of All Experience; Being Aware of Being Aware (The Essence of Meditation Series)

[10] Bill Plotkin: Soulcraft: Crossing into the Mysteries of Nature and Psyche; Nature and the Human Soul: Cultivating Wholeness and Community in a Fragmented World

According to Rupert Spira, this infinite realm of being is "Pure Consciousness". I felt very strong resonance with this perspective and felt that what he was referencing was synonymous with "spirit". In combination with the inspiration I drew from Bill Plotkin's work, specifically the book *Nature and the Human Soul*, I began to understand for myself that spirit, consciousness, and nature were ultimately one and the same—I felt that each could describe the infinite realm of all being and becoming.

So where do we find the soul within this infinite realm? In its sphere—its location, or its unique space. Metaphorically, we might say that the soul's place is a territory within spirit-consciousness-nature. Each of us has a unique soul sphere, and it is purely for us to explore and embody it in the course of our life. It encompasses the full potential of our entire being and becoming, on all levels—body, mind, heart, and spirit. From this perspective, our soul and our highest purpose are identical and are an inseparable part of the greater whole, the infinite realm of all being and becoming. Another way of understanding soul is to view it as the unique potential that is waiting to be explored and embodied by each of us.

Early in our lives we might not be aware of the potential of our soul. When any one of us is at the right place in our personal journey through life, we may start to sense that there is more to life than what meets the eye and the brain. Turning our awareness inward, we begin exploring and embodying this greater potential—our purpose, and the way we express ourselves as one distinct part of the wholeness of nature.

This transition can be very different for each of us. For me, I would describe it as the most difficult *and* the most rewarding experience of my life. It has been underway for many years, and I wouldn't dare to say that I have fully arrived. I don't know if we can ever finish exploring the entire potential of our soul. This is one of the wonderful mysteries of life.

Personal growth and the exploration of the soul are non-linear processes. Through these processes, we become aware of increasing perspectives and possibilities for choice in our lives. Seeing those increasing possibilities of choice is one expression of personal growth. As we go through life, our experiences enable us to add and/or shift perspectives, which means shifting the way we look at things. This mental and emotional flexibility supports us to add to or change the stories we tell about life and about what we believe in.

These processes make up the journey of soul exploration—a journey through a wide and mysterious territory. Once we become aware of a new part of that territory, we have the choice to embrace that part and use whatever resources it has to offer, or to make a different choice. This can look like going back to a territory with which we are more familiar, where we have already spent some time settling in. This is broadly defined as our comfort zone. Depending on our context and circumstances, we will subconsciously or consciously choose which of our experiences—old or new—will guide our actions and behaviors.

It took me quite a while to see and understand what it means to have the level of choice, and consequently the level of self-responsibility, that this understanding triggers. A specific experience opened my eyes.

Many years ago I attended a workshop on Holotropic Breathwork, which is a breathing practice that is intended to help with emotional healing and personal growth. It can bring you into an altered state of awareness, enabling you to access experiences that you presumably cannot access in a waking state. The method was developed by Stanislav Grof, a psychiatrist and one of the developers of Transpersonal Psychology. He used Breathwork as a successor to his LSD-based psychedelic therapy after the use of LSD was banned in the 1960s.

Letting go of control was scary to me at the time, so I needed to overcome some fears before attending the workshop. Once I jumped in, I was gifted with an indescribably wonderful experience. I literally felt like I was out of this world. I experienced myself as a beautiful, colorful, tropical bird, flying over a tropical forest filled with the most beautiful flowers, trees, and animals and the most incredible waterfalls. I was free, gliding up and down. I was taking in the joy, the ease, the beauty of it all. It felt completely real, and it felt like my first experience of true happiness.

After it was over, though I wasn't fully aware of it at the time, I had a choice: to either continue to explore where this experience had come from and what it told me about myself, or to merely remember the feelings of awe, joy, and happiness and leave it at that. I decided for the latter. I was not yet ready to dig deeper. Eventually the memory of this experience faded. Only when I heard or read about Holotropic Breathwork did the memory come back, as a thought like, "I know this. I experienced it once. It's great!".

Years later, while doing my JournaLogue practice, I had an inner dialogue with the part of me that I call "Inner Wisdom". The conversation was about my relationship with my creative potential. Throughout my life, I have been strongly drawn to many different forms of art; singing, dancing, painting, photography and eventually writing. At the same time, I was unconsciously limited by an underlying belief that none of my creative expressions were "good art". Through my JournaLogue, I was able to see and summarize this belief I was holding in one sentence: "I am not an artist."

After having become aware of this, the sequence of feelings whenever I did something that I identified as "creative" became clearer to me. First my mind and body relaxed, and I felt as though art was flowing through me. I became a channel through which something that wanted to emerge could manifest. This was then immediately followed by my belief system kicking in again. My thoughts arose: "just because I like it and enjoy doing it, that doesn't make it art."

In dialogue with my Inner Wisdom, I identified a part of me that Caroline Myss would describe as the "wounded child"—an aspect of the Child Archetype we all are holding within us. I had done a lot of shadow work with my wounded child, but I met a new aspect of it that now wanted to be seen. Establishing a relationship and dialogue with this inner child, I began to learn about its origins.

As children my sisters and I were expected to *be good*, which meant following the very rigid behavior norms defined by our parents. "Children are to be seen, not to be heard," was a sentence repeated many times in my childhood. What a story! Some of my elder sisters suffered severe punishments for behaving "badly", and although I was spared this level of abuse I still felt a lot of fear connected with not following the guidelines.

I learned very early that whenever I expressed my liveliness, playfulness, and creativity, I was behaving outside those defined behavior norms. I was called naughty, which translated into being a "bad girl". "Being naughty" triggered anger in my parents that felt like rejection and was very painful to me. The only way I saw to get some positive attention was to be a "good girl" by behaving as I was expected to. I developed a classical survival mechanism, which was to shut down my "naughty"—creative, playful, joyful—side, and turn into a sweet, well-behaved, yet somewhat repressed girl.

It wasn't until I could establish an inner dialogue about this experience that I discovered the connection between my naughty child and my lack of trust in my creative potential. Through my JournaLogue practice I built a relationship with my naughty child, and in the process of visualizing this part of my being it turned into a beautiful, colorful, tropical bird. The recognition was immediate. It was the same bird I had experienced with Holotropic Breathwork so many years earlier. Now I understood: this bird is my creativity. I was moved to tears.

Years prior, through the altered state of awareness that Holotropic Breathwork induces, my subconscious had spoken to me, but at the time I chose not to explore the meaning of the experience. I am sure it was a good choice then. I wasn't ready to face this aspect of my wounded inner child, but the moment when I finally became ready was the moment my creativity was liberated.

After this I could look back and recognize moments in my life when I didn't include my creativity, or when I began to follow my creative intuition but didn't quite trust myself to actually go through with it. This lack of trust reduced my power and weakened my embodiment of creative intuition.

Since then, I have developed a very different relationship to my Creativity. She is now a regular part of my daily JournaLogue practice, which means that I can dialogue with her any time to get her input on any question.

I think this story is a good example of the non-linearity of the processes of personal growth and exploring our soul. When I decided to experience Holotropic Breathwork, I was looking for something that would help me understand myself better. Though I didn't have a clear understanding at the time, I now know that I was looking to explore new "soul territory". I experienced what was available for me to manifest in my life, but it wasn't until years later that I became able to return to this territory, or this aspect of me and integrate it. This yielded an entirely new capacity for creative freedom in my life.

Maria, a JournaLogue client, shared another example with me. As a business consultant and coach, her passion was to teach empathy and compassion in teams. Like so many, Maria had experienced her childhood as very difficult—even traumatic. She had done a great deal of work on her own personal development to resolve that pain, and consequently built loving relationships with most of her family members. Only in interactions with two family members did she continue to be pulled back into dysfunctional, painful dynamics of blaming and shaming.

For years, Maria felt that the only way to stay out of these dynamics was to avoid contact in general. She knew the "territory" where empathy and compassion were available as resources, and they had already enabled so much healing, but in the specific contexts of her relationships with these two family members she simply couldn't access these resources yet. Finally, on a fasting and silence retreat, a new insight revealed itself and Maria could heal these two relationships as well. With this breakthrough, tools that had been useless suddenly worked to resolve some of the most painful relationships in her life.

Today, Maria reports that she has healthy relationships with these two family members, centered in her own internal capacity for balancing empathy and compassion with self-understanding and healthy boundaries.

Through my quest to understand the source of our personal purpose, I came to understand three things for myself:

1. Our highest purpose is identical with our soul potential, and

2. To explore our purpose is to explore the "territory" of our unique sphere/location/space within pure spirit-consciousness-nature, and

3. this soul exploration is a non-linear journey, and one that we can only take when ready.

States

Pure thought and contemplation are insufficient for the journey of exploring the soul. My experience with Holotropic Breathwork and my meditation-induced experience of connectedness with everything are both examples of soul exploration that transcend thought. Through my JournaLogue practice I've come to innumerable realizations, and I've been gifted with additional insight through powerful dreams.

Some call the states through which we can explore our soul "states of consciousness", but with the definition of consciousness I've learned to embrace, I prefer to call them "states of awareness".

We can experience awareness while awake, in what Rupert Spira calls "the waking state of mind". Even while awake, we can be in different states, such as daydreaming or shock.

We can experience sleep states—light sleep, deep sleep, or REM sleep—often called the dream phase. We can also be unconscious, hypnotized, in a coma, or in trance. We can access different states through spiritual practices like meditation and prayer, or through physical practices like athletics and yoga. Intimacy, sexuality, and relationships can induce state experiences, as can the use of substances like psychedelics, alcohol and drugs. Holotropic Breathwork, described above, leads to another state of awareness.

Each state offers different pathways and experiences. In our waking state of mind, we tend to be aware of experiences through our physical sensations—seeing, hearing, feeling, tasting, and smelling. While awake, we can also be aware of our thoughts and emotions. As we shift into states such as sleep, meditation, or another induced state, our experiences change.

The less awake we are, the less control our cognitive processes have over our experiences. One might say that the less awake we are, the more freedom of experience we have. Knowing about states of awareness and learning to intentionally access different states is an important part of exploring the territory of our soul.

Bill Plotkin calls this process "soul encounter". In his book *Soulcraft* he writes that there are two phases for us to go through: "1) learning and employing techniques for soul encounter, practices that will help us approach the soul and gather what we find there, and 2) cultivating a soulful relationship to our life, and to all life".

Plotkin's book includes an extensive list of tools and practices, such as dream work, journal work, fasting, breath work, the enactment of traditional ceremonies, rituals, and nature festivals, yoga disciplines, symbolic artwork, vision questing, skillful use of hallucinogenic substances within sacred ceremonies, and others.

Once we decide we are ready for the journey, each of us can find our own set of tools and practices that enable us to explore our soul in different states of awareness. As shown with the example of my beautiful tropical bird, when we are ready the meanings of these experiences become accessible to us in our waking state of mind. We can then think about and express what we understand, while we are awake: speak it, write it, sing it, dance it, or form, draw, or paint it. We express our discoveries about our soul in whatever ways feel right to us.

My own understanding of "soul"—that which is uniquely mine, located in the sphere of all being and becoming that is spirit-consciousness-nature—leads me to a clear definition of purpose.

Purpose is the calling to bring one's gift forward—embodying and expressing the highest potential of what one's soul can offer to the world.

Purpose alignment

With an understanding of our own personal purpose—that which we can identify and name in waking life, at least—we can make more intentional decisions and choices and let it guide all aspects of our life. When it comes to the question about where and how we invest our energy, time, and talent to do our work in the world, we develop a need for purpose alignment.

I have been gifted by the experience of working with a number of people with whom I felt deep purpose alignment, which led to some of the most meaningful friendships of my life. Those relationships were and are beautiful and important, and they aren't just all laughs, hugs, joy, and harmony. These relationships have also called for sometimes difficult processing of inter- and intra-personal conflicts.

That in itself isn't so special. We all grow *in* and *with* relationships in which we work through our personal differences. In community with other "Purpose Agents"—the collective of people engaged in a purpose-guided company, thus all serving the same purpose that was larger than any one of us individually—this work goes deeper. In such a collective, we agreed to acknowledge that each of our actions were rooted in purpose and that we would therefore always hold each other in positive regard. We agreed that, when triggered by the behavior of another, we would avoid going into patterns of judging, blaming, or shaming, but to inquire about the deeper reasoning of that specific behavior. This inquiry, as difficult as it often was, required us to practice empathy and to see and understand things from the perspective of the other. Naturally this led us to understanding one another on a much deeper level, to get clarity on our expectations towards each other and, if necessary, to find new agreements about these expectations.

Understanding purpose as the way our soul expresses itself at any given moment of our life brings an entirely new level of appreciation for the importance of purpose to every single one of us. Experiencing how this shapes the relationships within a collective of people engaging together for a company's purpose, larger than each member of the collective, I dare say that the capacity of a purpose-aligned collective to move things forward in service to a larger purpose gives rise to a whole new level of potential.

Purpose alignment, or the resonance and proximity of our own personal purpose with the purpose of another person or a system, is of vital necessity for any purpose-guided endeavor. It supports us individually and collectively to remain focused and oriented towards fulfilling purpose. On an individual level, awareness of our personal purpose and its evolution is a prerequisite for aligning with a system's purpose. We feel purpose-aligned when what we are doing serves something larger than ourselves, while at the same time letting us embody and manifest our individual purpose. A collective that serves a larger purpose must be composed of members who are each personally purpose-aligned, at least to some degree. Even though each member has a unique individual purpose, alignment lets them simultaneously care and engage for the same larger purpose.

Reflecting on my struggles with the shift into self-organization, and on the struggles I witnessed in many of my clients, I realized that there is more to purpose alignment than merely being aware of our own purpose and finding resonance with the purpose of a company or entity. To be part of a purpose aligned collective, it is particularly helpful to understand *surrender* and *agency*.

Surrender

The word "surrender" often triggers a sense of waving the white flag, being the loser, or giving up and handing off power to others. The form of surrender that I've learned to understand, guided by my own and by a larger purpose, is very different. The form of surrender I am talking about feels like an essential part of our personal development journey into leading a purpose-guided life.

This is a difficult journey, because ultimately surrender means letting go. Letting go of our attachment to specific beliefs. Letting go of desired outcomes. We let go of our preconceived ideas about how things should be, about what is right and what is wrong. We let go of control and open up to what wants to be. We open up to the realm of not knowing.

What I found so difficult to learn was that surrendering doesn't mean giving myself up in service of something else. I needed to learn that the answer to what is needed in any given moment lies in the space in between, or the space of the unknown, and that I am as important a part of this space as are others and the surrounding context.

Surrender lies in allowing the unfolding from the space in between.

My learning journey around surrender began when I realized that I repeatedly ran into situations where I felt triggered by the behavior of someone else and reacted by letting myself fully into a conflict-laden discussion. I had a habit of saying clearly what I thought was wrong about the other person's perspective and defending what I felt was right. When I was invited to hold the other person in positive regard and to remember that we all act from purpose, it became clear that I needed to let go of my habitual behavior.

The process of letting go of this behavior was one of the hardest stages of my personal development journey. Often, it took me right back into my childhood and consequently asked me to work with my shadows. These brought up a line of stories that I could see from a new perspective, and that I needed to integrate.

As a child I experienced my family situation as an environment that lacked love. Not feeling loved led me to feeling unimportant, unworthy of attention, unworthy of love, and unworthy of so much. I am sure you have heard that story many times. I don't consider this part of my story as unique in any way, but the sad commonality of difficult childhoods doesn't make exploring and seeing these feelings any less painful.

Like all children in emotional pain, I needed to develop a strategy that would help me cope with this pain. My survival strategy, like most, developed on its own without rational thought. It came from the motivation that I had to develop a behavior that would get me seen and heard—one that would give me the sense of having a place, or a sense of belonging. Being a good, well-behaved girl had helped me up to a point, but once I was out of the "cute little girl" stage, it wasn't enough anymore. It helped me to survive, but not to develop a sense of being worthy. I needed to find a different way to be acknowledged and loved.

Quite unconsciously, I began to develop a sense of my intelligence. At some point during childhood, I began to feel that a "sharp mind" would be acknowledged. Trying to identify the seed of this feeling brings back a story from when I was about seven or eight years old. The sister closest to me in age and I were an inseparable duo in our early childhood, as we still are today. Though inseparable, we had the most terrible fights: yelling, screaming, hitting each other, crying. Our conflict could be quite brutal.

My sister, being older and taller, had always been the winner. I don't know where it came from, but one day when we began to fight again, I stood up in front of her, crossed my arms, and launched a stoic verbal defense. I said things like, "I don't care". "Hit me and see if I care", "I don't care what you say". "Go ahead, it won't change anything". Outwardly, I presented myself as completely calm. I recall that she completely freaked out, but if I remember correctly that interaction didn't lead to a physical fight. It was the first time I came out of a fight feeling like I had won. I remember it as the day that our big fights ended. This was the place where I began to learn to cut myself off from my feelings, bringing my whole energy into my head. *This* would help me be the winner.

From that day on, I perfected how to cut myself off from my feelings and to use words like weapons—razor sharp and geared towards winning. As you may imagine, this didn't get me love, but it did get me the feeling that I was being noticed.

I didn't use my intelligence for academic achievements. I was a terrible student, going through school without putting in a lot of effort and getting very bad grades. And, by the time I graduated from high school I was an infamous arguer. I had developed my use of emotionless, razor-sharp rhetoric to a very high level.

Reflecting on my pattern of dealing with conflict brought up these early stories and led me to visualizing my pattern. What came up in a group therapy session where we worked with systemic constellations, was a very disturbing image. I could see myself standing tall, with a thick iron plate or blade going through my throat and resting on my shoulders—almost like a guillotine. This iron plate made sure that my brain—my intellectual capacity—and my feelings were safely separated.

Once I had overcome the shock of this image, I could visualize removing the blade. With it gone, I felt reborn. This healing opened up a whole new sense of life flowing within and through me. From that day on, I had to completely relearn how to connect and communicate with others when different perspectives were present.

This learning supported me in behaving *differently*, but it didn't immediately support me in behaving *effectively*. At first, when I felt confronted or triggered by different perspectives, I would pull back and not say anything at all. I simply didn't know how to deal with this mix of emotions and perspectives and this new, far more complex "me" showing up. Two things, in combination, eventually helped me to open up and trust that it was safe to add my perspective to the mix. First, I had trusting and supportive relationships with the people I worked with. Second, I leaned on the explicit agreements we had with each other: to hold each other in positive regard, to understand that we are all acting from purpose; and to seek to understand individual differences through inquiring with care, compassion and concern.

Within that container, I was able to rewrite old habits and let go of many beliefs and preconceptions about myself, about relationships, about control, about collaboration, about meaning making, and so much more. I could open up to the realm of not knowing and to what wants to be. I learned what it really means to surrender. It doesn't mean giving yourself up, but quite the contrary:

> **Surrender means bringing your whole self to be of service, individually and collectively. To be of service to your own purpose, to a larger purpose, and ultimately to the greater whole.**

Being part of a purpose-aligned collective means surrendering not to the collective, but to the *responsibility for* the collective. If a choice is needed, interest for the collective generally comes before your individual interest. If the choice is difficult, there might be a lack of alignment. If that lack of alignment continues over time, this could be a sign of decreasing purpose alignment. This isn't in itself bad—it just means that the resonance and proximity of your personal purpose with the larger purpose that the collective is serving may have decreased. Perhaps one or both of the purposes have evolved, and it might be time for you to make a change—to find stronger purpose alignment through doing something else.

When the workplace begins to feel less attractive and the work less satisfying, people often turn to searching for something, or even someone, to blame for these feelings. When acting from the awareness of purpose alignment, we can see that we are embedded in constant evolution of everything, including ourselves. While blaming keeps us focused on specific causes for our discomfort, reflecting on purpose and purpose alignment opens our awareness to what is up next for us and lets us surrender to this divine process.

Agency

While learning to understand the importance and relevance of surrender, I repeatedly encountered the dilemma of choice. For example, I might feel the need to understand if my next action will serve my own interest, or the interest of the collective that I'm part of. This can be confusing when those two interests seem to contradict each other. Similarly, I might feel torn between acting on behalf of my personal purpose or on behalf of a systemic purpose, such as that of a company I am engaging with. Even with a high sense of purpose alignment, this can still happen. As an example, an ethical vegan employed by an educational nonprofit might feel confused about whether her strong advocacy for a shift toward plant-based cafeteria service comes from her personal purpose to reduce animal suffering, or to the organization's purpose to educate people. While she could make arguments in favor of the latter, she recognizes that her personal purpose may skew her decisions away from pure service to the purpose of the nonprofit she cares so much about.

Watching many clients face similar dilemmas, I became aware that resolving those dilemmas felt really difficult in some cases, while in others the resolution came with a sense of contentment, ease, and flow in moving forward. What was the difference? While being conscious of purpose alignment and surrender, why do some decisions about how to best serve purpose sometimes leave one feeling incomplete, while others create a sense of joy and satisfaction?

The difference is **agency**. The following story from a client gives an example of what it means and why it's so important.

Edward, a co-founder of a social enterprise offering sound technology and music production services for disadvantaged youth, asked me to coach him through such a dilemma. His personal purpose was "meaningful connections around the globe". He was very passionate about connecting young people from different walks of life and different parts of the world to learn *about* and *from* one another, and through doing so he sought to create more global understanding and compassion.

Co-founding his company gave Edward one pathway to express his purpose through music. The company's purpose was about enabling young musicians with disadvantaged backgrounds (refugees, the educationally-underserved, and youth with historically marginalized identities or special needs) to bring their music to the world through inexpensive or free online music production services.

Through his work, Edward realized that something was deeply missing—the opportunity for disadvantaged young people to receive lessons or coaching. While the self-taught musicians who arrived to record music were grateful for the recording opportunity, Edward realized just how much more their lives and musical careers could be transformed if they were also matched with instructors for free or reduced cost lessons. While others in the company agreed that music lessons would unlock more potential for those they served, they largely felt that it was not this company's work to provide education.

This was a huge dilemma for Edward, and he felt that he could only resolve his dilemma through an either/or decision—found a new company, or drop the tension and continue with the work he was already doing. He decided to continue engaging in his company as before. He told me that he felt it was a good decision, but something felt off. He just couldn't shake off the feeling of letting someone down.

The decision of the company not to add music lessons to their services presented Edward with a dilemma. He felt something missing for him, for the company, and for the young people who would benefit from the education he envisioned. He sought coaching to understand where he had agency to act—and to understand if he had a pathway forward other than resigning from the company and starting a new one.

In our coaching sessions we explored Edward's sense of purpose alignment. He understood that the decision made in his self-organized company *against* offering musical education came through a decision-making process he and his colleagues had all agreed upon, and he knew he needed to surrender to it. Nonetheless, he also sensed a really important need that he deeply wanted to serve. We discussed why this was so important to him, even though he loved the work he was already doing, and this question motivated him to explore his current purpose.

Through coaching around purpose, Edward discovered the word "healing" as a missing part of his expression of personal purpose. His new purpose of "healing connections around the globe." Through his purpose quest he had remembered how art had helped him connect to himself and to others and heal from trauma. "Healing" opened a whole new depth of meaning for Edward. He had seen more of his soul.

With this new clarity, Edward was ready to make decisions without a feeling of either/or, or of letting anything or anyone down. He shifted his engagement with his current company to half time, and before long found two collaborators with whom to co-found a new company to heal trauma through arts and arts education.

Edward's experience shows how surrender and agency support us to stay purpose aligned. Edward started out believing that he was clear on his own purpose and the company's purpose, and he knew that he needed to surrender to the fact that what was important to him wasn't necessarily important to others or to the organization, even despite a high degree of purpose alignment.

What kept Edward moving forward was his capacity to navigate the dilemma of surrender and agency; of surrendering by accepting the decision of his company, while at the same time staying true to what was calling him and acting on it. The end result was great for everything, and everyone involved: Edward's first company and the people engaged in it, the need for arts education and the new company serving this need, the people who engaged for *that* purpose, and—especially—the youth served by both companies.

So, what is agency?

Agency is a concept discussed and debated in many different disciplines ranging from sociology and psychology to philosophy and spirituality. There are many definitions. In all of the literature out there, there are no definitions of agency that resonate with my personal experience and that of those I've worked with. Here's how I define it:

Agency is the drive to express our personal purpose with awareness and autonomy, and with integrity to who we truly are at any given moment in time.

With agency, we make meaningful and clear decisions and act with self-trust and wisdom. Our actions are rooted in our purpose. Bringing agency to our decisions to engage with and serve one or more systemic purposes (of a company, a network, a community, a movement, an institution) enables us to sense into and have awareness of the degree to which we are purpose-aligned.

Holding the necessity for both surrender and agency will bring us into dilemmas. The beautiful thing about this is that these dilemmas invite us to "dance" with them, to move in their in-between space, to be with and available for what can emerge from this space. We dance here until the space gives rise to clarity on the next step that is needed.

Your manifestation of purpose

Whether there is clarity to express it or not, each person on this planet has a purpose. Using the metaphor of our souls being a location, a territory within the realm of infinite being and becoming, we can develop a sense of awareness how we are all ultimately connected through our source, whether we call it spirit, consciousness, or nature.

At this point I would like to invite you to a short reflection. You may even use these questions as prompts for journaling:

- What is your current answer to the question, "what is your purpose?"

- How is your personal purpose currently expressing itself in your life?

- Looking back, did your purpose change and become more clear over time? If so, describe how.

- To what extent are your decisions and actions guided by your purpose?
- To what extent do you feel purpose alignment with what you do professionally?
- How do surrender and agency show up for you?
- Is something in the way of you fully expressing your purpose?

Getting to know ever more of our soul means getting to know what wants to manifest through us. In this way we are invited to be of service to the realm of infinite being and becoming; in all aspects of our life, from day to day, from moment to moment.

When this clarity first began to emerge for me, I felt completely overwhelmed. It felt so enormously big, but over time I found out that it isn't about this enormously big thing at all. Each of us can contribute in our own way, and our own way doesn't have a measure. It isn't big, it isn't small—it just is.

Some Resources for Personal Purpose Quests

Bill Plotkin: **Soulcraft**: *Crossing into the Mysteries of Nature and Psyche;* New World Library; 9.10.2003 edition (August 29, 2003)

Tim Kelley: **True Purpose**: *12 Strategies for Discovering the Difference You Are Meant to Make;* Transcendent Solutions Press; First Edition (April 1, 2009)

Emanuel Kuntzelman: **Purpose Rising:** *A Global Movement of Transformation and Meaning; Bright Alliance (October 10, 2017)*

Bill Plotkin: **Journey of Soul Initiation**: *A Field Guide for Visionaries, Evolutionaries, and Revolutionaries;* New World Library (January 12, 2021)

Manifesting our purpose can show up in the way we hold our children, treat our loved ones, treat ourselves, prepare our food, support others, do work, walk in a meadow, allow stillness, embrace noise, play, sleep—you name it. Everything we do can be a manifestation of purpose, no matter how small or big it might appear to us.

The story of power

Manifesting our personal purpose means serving the greater whole. It means being true to who we are, to our soul. Everyone who is aware of their personal purpose, in one way or another, longs to manifest it in their lives. Many people, however, see reasons why manifesting their purpose isn't possible.

This brings us back to questions about what is holding us back: fear and overwhelm. When it comes to manifesting purpose, what lies underneath the fear and overwhelm?

Over the past decade I have facilitated hundreds of people in a reflection process that is part of the *Language of Spaces*[11] (LoS) framework. This framework offers content and practices to develop the core capacities to thrive in a self-organized context. The process helps people find pathways to process and resolve tensions they are sensing, but are not sure about how to move forward. It supports them in differentiating and reflecting on their tension from different perspectives including—among others—its relational, or interpersonal aspects, and its individual, or intra-personal aspects. Many of the tensions brought by my clients are grounded in the complex and faceted challenges of manifesting personal purpose.

---

[11] http://www.languageofspaces.org

> Language of Spaces
>
> The Language of Spaces (LoS) framework combines essential theories, principles, and practices to support individuals and collectives to develop the 4 core capacities needed to thrive within a self-organized context:
>
> - Differentiation & Integration
> - Purpose Alignment
> - Self-Realization
> - Inner Leadership
>
> LoS fosters awareness and processing of personal and organizational tensions required for, and leading to, evolutionary growth.

Though each LoS process is unique, over time I could see a pattern. One significant issue showed up in nearly every process: fear, and/or overwhelm, rooted in a story we tell ourselves about power. This often feels like a story of others having power over us or of our being expected (by ourselves or by others) to exert power over others. This can be a story about losing power, about feeling powerless, about having power, about empowerment, about stepping into authentic power, or about the misuse of power—by ourselves or by others. There is almost no limit to the ways stories of power challenge us.

As I was beginning to see this relationship between power and fear and/or overwhelm as an obstacle for many people yearning to lead a purpose-guided and meaningful life, something else came up. In the work I and others were doing at encode.org, the term "PowerShift" emerged. It helped to show more clearly that shifting the relationship we personally have with power was a key part of the work of encode.org, in service to its purpose: "to connect power, purpose, and work". The work was, and is, manifested in defining the For-Purpose Enterprise[12], which defines new structures, processes, and agreements for all contexts of an enterprise: the structural organizational context, the legal and financial context, and the people context with its inter- and intra-personal dynamics.

A For-Purpose Enterprise is a truly distributed system. It distributes purpose, authority, decision making, and ownership, redefines investment, and enables work without employment to break up the employer/employee dependency. As encode.org embraced the term PowerShift, it defined the power shift as going from "power over" to "power with".

Though this concept was radically new and involved big experimentation, it was at the same time very concrete. The system is based in a set of written, agreed upon, and evolutionary agreements: an Operating Agreement that defines the Holacracy Constitution as the agreement in the *Organization Context*, a dynamic system of ownership based on Mike Moyer's "Slicing Pie" model and other important legal aspects in the *Company Context*, and the Association Agreement in the *People Context*.

Despite the complexity of the Operating Agreement and the steep learning curve to work with Holacracy for those who joined us and were new to it, encode.org navigated the Company and the Organization Context really well. In my experience, there was more difficulty in the People Context, the space to deal with our relationships with one another and with ourselves.

In the case of an interpersonal conflict, we could rely on one another to process in an open, empathetic, and compassionate way. For me this led to friendships with many of my colleagues, with a depth and quality I had never experienced before in the context of work.

Though our Association Agreement helped us at encode.org to navigate our interpersonal relationships well, I felt that something

---

[12] Jo Aschenbrenner: *The For-Purpose Enterprise: A Powershifted Operating System to Run Your Business*; tredition; 1st edition (2 Nov. 2020)

was missing. Sometimes I found myself falling into dysfunctional behavior patterns, like blaming someone for things I considered had gone "wrong" (in other words, not the way I wanted them to go), or asking for permission—in sometimes subtle ways—when there was absolutely nothing I needed to ask permission for. Sometimes I felt frustrated or hurt but lacked the courage to address it. I could also observe others struggling with their level of autonomy and with the dilemma of agency and surrender.

Linda Berens, a colleague at encode.org, repeatedly pointed us to questions about the collective. Linda is a thought leader in the world of psychological type, developer of the InterStrength™ CORE Approach (see textbox) and founder of InterStrength Institute (https://www.interstrength.org), and she among others shared my sense that something more was needed to support our work together.

> The InterStrength™ CORE Approach helps us know ourselves and understand others in a way that honors individual differences and helps us understand and claim our own power. It involves a self-discovery process that uses integrated multiple models that inform us of our core Essential Motivators, Interaction Styles, and Intentional Drivers. This approach fosters a deep understanding and self-awareness that restores our love and appreciation of ourselves and of others.

Despite our clear Association Agreement, tensions within the collective showed up in tough discussions with an energy of "right and wrong" and brought some very painful interpersonal conflicts. These were difficult, sometimes even impossible to resolve. As is the nature of experimentation, things could get messy.

Reflecting on times when I'd fallen into patterns of blaming, asking for permission, or even holding back, I recognized a sense of disconnection from myself in those moments. This disconnection made me feel weak, as though I'd lost my personal power. I began to understand that even though my colleagues and I, like many of my clients, were working in a system of distributed authority, this didn't automatically mean that we were working with distributed *power*.

Introspection on the subject of personal power took me back to the story I shared about learning to trust my Creativity. In my JournaLogue practice, I asked, "when do I feel strong, grounded, and most connected to my authentic power?" Surprisingly, the answer came from my Creativity: "When you trust and express life through me." I remembered learning about trusting my Creativity and seeing that not trusting her had made me weak. In an ongoing dialogue, my Creativity told me something important.

"If you don't trust that your life is your unique and authentic creation from moment to moment, then you can't trust life as a whole."

From somewhere in the unexplored depths of myself came a feeling of discomfort while contemplating about trusting life through trusting my Creativity. It felt almost as if something or someone was forbidding me to live a powerful, creative life. But who, or what, was forbidding it?

I kept searching. I asked my Creativity in which forms she showed up in my life. She told me, "I connect that which wants to emerge to your awareness. You can call it intuition, imagination, originality, or authenticity—I bring it into your awareness, and I point you towards the manifestation, the doing. Creativity is being and doing, otherwise it is like an empty shell."

As much as I had learned to trust my Creativity, there was a gap between letting something emerge into my awareness and actually going through with it. Disconnecting from myself (blaming, asking for permission, or holding back) was my strategy to avoid expressing my Creativity, to stop between awareness and acting on what wanted to be expressed through me. In this hesitation, I disempowered myself. But why?

I meditated, visualized, and journaled while holding the question, "what would my life be like if I allowed myself to fully trust and manifest my Creativity?"

Never before had it been so hard for me to go into these contemplative practices. My mind kept racing in all different directions. I couldn't calm down, no matter how many breathing exercises I did. I can't remember how many attempts I made before I could let go of fear and control enough that "it" could come out of the shadows, but then it happened.

What follows is a description of a vision I experienced during meditation that includes harmful, false beliefs about indigeneity—I'll share it here as I experienced it, with the humility to recognize that my upbringing and socialization steeped me in worldviews that historically have created and presently still are creating toxicity through racism and supremacy.

Words, images, and sounds emerged. Words like primitive, wild, savages, driven by uncontrolled urges, simple, brutes. I saw crowds of Neanderthals, as well as people from contemporary indigenous cultures: Africans in the bush, Native Americans, Australian Aboriginals. There was noise—so much loud noise! Drumming, chanting, laughing, yelling, and screaming. There was so much movement—running, dancing, fighting, killing. In my vision, this was all happening at the same time and was frightening to the point that it felt almost life threatening.

It was the most frightening experience I ever had during any contemplative practice, and I went into shock. My whole body was shaking, I was sobbing, my heart was racing, I was sweating and freezing at the same time, and I thought I was going to throw up.

The realization hit me: somewhere deep down in my shadow, I was connected to a belief that expressing my life through pure and authentic Creativity, through my intuitive wisdom, was like being a "primitive, uneducated, savage". While I would never have consciously judged indigeneity as "less than" or "frightening," those who showed up in my visualization did wild things and were driven by uncontrolled urges. My deeply entrenched belief was revealing itself: that these unleashed behaviors were despicable, and needed to be tamed, educated, or civilized. I had an ingrained belief that I couldn't allow myself to live with that level of freedom.

It took days until the shock began to subside and until I could think about this experience without immediately starting to shiver and cry again. At first, I simply couldn't understand why all this had come up at this moment, when I only wanted to understand more about how power connected to self-organization.

Was I really this horribly judgmental, racist person, driven by principles of supremacy? I felt more disconnected from myself, struggling with judging, even hating myself for this insight. I turned all the derogatory thoughts and feelings that had come up in my visualization against myself.

Connection and dialogue with my Inner Wisdom helped me get through this. I kept receiving the message, "stay with it. You can do it. You can go through this experience until you can see what it is really about."

A journey through my lineage

As hard as it was, I stayed with questions about the meaning of my troubling vision, and I even participated in a retreat to support me in my quest. There, I was invited to walk into the surrounding woods and choose a tree, to sit with it, to connect to it, and to ask it to talk to me as a representative of my ancestral lineage.

This took me on yet another of my most impactful introspection journeys. After breathing with the tree for a while, I saw an image emerge on its bark. It invited me in. I felt myself walking back through history, walking past my parents and grandparents, further and further, I saw many people that I didn't know, but felt connected to. There were many adults and even more children of all ages. Everyone was motionless, stuck in a specific body posture. Some had laughing faces, others were crying, some had faces twisted with pain, anger, or hatred. Some were standing, others sitting alone or in groups. Some crouched, others were stuck in postures of dancing, running, or walking. I walked through beautiful countryside, dark woods, crowded streets, and houses both majestic and humble. I passed through parks dotted with beautiful flowers, over lawns between people sitting on picnic blankets, and through muddy swamps in the pouring rain. Then, as in a horror movie, I began to see graveyards and caskets. I saw weapons—guns, cannons, and grenades. I walked over battlefields with dead bodies all around me.

Eventually I walked back towards my grandparents and parents, and as I approached them, our surroundings faded until there was nothing, absolutely nothing, around them. It looked as if my relatives were surrounded by fog or smoke, with no ground to stand on. They were floating in this dark sphere. I studied their faces and body postures very carefully, until I finally got it: they were completely lost.

I could see that my grandparents' and parents' lives, on both sides of the family, had been dominated by loss. Looking at my grandparents, all born in the 19th century, and my parents, born in the early 1920s, I could painfully feel all they'd been through. The loss of their countries, through the fall of the Austro-Hungarian Monarchy, the formation of Czechoslovakia, and occupation as part of the communist Eastern Bloc in what is now the Czech Republic. Losses from both the first and second World Wars. Loss of children and siblings, loss of homes, loss of freedom, loss of social status, loss of identity, loss of dignity, loss of family properties, loss of family businesses, loss of connection between and among parents, children, and siblings, loss of marriages, and loss of things beyond my ability to know.

As soon as I understood that I was looking at a collective story of loss, more and more people began to appear and join my family in this mist. The crowd grew to hundreds, thousands, then millions of people—a never-ending crowd. It was obvious that all were holding this crushing feeling of loss. I could see and feel it: I was in the middle of a collective trauma. I could feel the physical and emotional pain. It brought me back to the shocking experience I had had in meditation, where I encountered my fear of fully expressing my creativity, heeding my intuition, and following the voice of my authenticity.

I understood now that my shocking experience had been an invitation to see a vast collective trauma, and to see myself as part of it. To see that this trauma was, and still is, caused by stories about power that humanity has developed and believed as truth.

Stories that tell how power is the means to prove who is stronger and who is weaker, who is the winner and who is the loser, who is right and who is wrong. Stories about who owns the truth. Stories about the "civilized" and "uncivilized" world. Stories that were, and are, used to justify all manner of atrocities: colonialization, slavery, exploitation, genocide, wars, dictatorships, injustice, abuse. Stories and resulting actions that cause unspeakable pain and loss.

Hearing my tree's leaves rustle in the wind, I emerged from my inner journey. I sat there seeing, with frightening clarity, one primary loss that humanity has created on its path. This one loss has cost us so much and caused us to do so many inhuman things. This is the loss of the interconnectedness of everything—our connection to self, to other, and to all.

The separation that comes with this loss enables judgment: mine is better, true, more valuable. We wield power over others to prove it. The story of separateness is the prerequisite to most other stories of power. If we hadn't created the story of separateness, we would see that what we do to other humans, we do to ourselves, and to humanity as a whole. What we do to nature, we do to ourselves, and to our planetary body. This shows up in collective trauma, and we are only beginning to understand what that really means for humanity and for the more-than-human world.

Connecting collective and personal trauma

The overwhelming magnitude of this experience—and my resulting reflections on collective trauma, my own family history, and my personal patterns—took some time and work to process, but I was able to find some comfort by coming back to reflect on my own patterns. With the new understanding I'd been given in my experience with the tree, I could see so much more clearly how I'd experienced my childhood, and how the traumatic stories of ongoing loss in my family and culture continued to play out in my life.

In reflecting on my childhood, I recognized the unconscious strategy I had developed to cope with loss. Based on the belief that nothing is here to stay, I subconsciously set myself up to avoid having anything in the first place that I might lose—thereby inadvertently recreating loss, again and again. In retrospect, I could see how this created a life of scarcity for me in so many ways. Romantic relationships were not there to stay, which led to a series of unhappy relationships that from the beginning were destined to end. Money was not there to stay—what a field in which to repeat my patterns! There was not an area in my life that wasn't touched by this mechanism to cope with loss. The ongoing journey of seeing and letting go of these patterns, which kept me recreating patterns of scarcity in my life, has been such a liberation!

While doing all this individual shadow work, I was still vividly aware of that large scale collective trauma I had witnessed in my vision. I saw my family's trauma as a small part of a much larger collective issue, and that it was directly connected to my quest to understand power.

American psychologist Peter Levine has worked as a specialist in the field of trauma for over 40 years. He said, "trauma also unites the world, because nobody gets away without having encounters with threat."

This quote precisely described my experience. Painful as it was, I took myself back into the visualization and returned to these millions of people in the mist. Using a technique that had helped me before, I then "zoomed out" to try and see a bigger picture. From this distance, I explored whether my sense of power as a root cause for so much of humanity's collective trauma, was holding.

"Trauma is not the event, it is the impact an event has on our body and its entire nervous system, and on our mind," according to Peter Levine. I could see all these horrible events in history that caused the trauma, events forced on one another through someone(s) feeling legitimized to hold power over others. I could see how in these experiences, people and communities feel overpowered and powerless, lacking the power to protect or defend themselves. This led me to an assumption.

All individual and collective traumas have a similar root cause: power over, wielded forcefully.

"Power over, wielded forcefully"—whether by a person, by a group of people, by a natural disaster, by an accident, or by a health issue—needs two sides: the side that wields the power and the side that lacks the means to stop this from happening. All these incidents are potential causes for individual or collective trauma.

In 2019, at a Science and Nonduality Conference[13] (SAND), Peter Levine connected in conversation with Thomas Hübl[14], a contemporary spiritual teacher and author who does wonderful work on collective and intergenerational trauma. In that conversation, Levine said, "the types of memory that are involved in trauma have nothing to do with conscious memory. They have nothing to do with the way a declarative memory is remembered. They are remembered in the body, the so-called procedure memories, as reaction patterns in our body and emotions that just erupt seemingly out of nowhere."

When learning about individual and collective trauma, the words fear and overwhelm come up a lot. Trauma is caused by a threat, which causes fear, and we feel overwhelmed by this threat because we don't have the power to avoid it or protect ourselves. Herein lay the connection to the patterns of fear and overwhelm I had encountered so often in my consulting work, and which we explored in Chapter 3.

When the issue of letting go of the story of "power over" is addressed, it often touches a nerve. This literally means it touches our nervous system, which is where the embodied memory of our traumas are located. Since addressing the power shift often is

---

[13] The Wisdom of Trauma: https://www.scienceandnonduality.com/the-wisdom-of-trauma
[14] https://thomashuebl.com/

understood as "letting go of power", it can leave us with a sense of powerlessness. Naturally, for anyone subject to personal or ancestral trauma at the hands of the more powerful, this is a fearful specter which would leave us completely defenseless. Assuming that those uninterested in power-shifting would then easily wield their power over us feels, to our trauma-impacted nervous systems, like a very real threat.

There is another power-related fear that works the other way around: the fear of becoming powerful. Marianne Williamson, a famous American author, spiritual leader, and political activist, says, "our deepest fear is not that we are inadequate. Our deepest fear is that we are powerful beyond measure." It's clear that the power she speaks of isn't "power over", but something profoundly different and profoundly tied to purpose. Authentic power is available to us when we let go of stories of power-over. This is the power to fully self-realize, through manifesting our purpose.

In a survey entitled, "Are You Manifesting Your Authentic Power?", I asked a number of questions around the topic of authentic power. The results confirmed my experience. There was not one participant who didn't at least once address fear, in relation to being authentic, and it was generally the fear of what might happen: rejection, ridicule, loss of community, loss of acceptance, or loss of employment. Some feared letting others down, and others feared having to make massive changes in every aspect of their current lives.

All this reinforced my assumption that the reaction patterns I had been experiencing were based on the unconscious "autopilot" that drives us, and that is rooted in collective trauma. For a new story about power to ripple out into the world, we need to deal with the collective trauma caused by the story of power over.

My intense personal experiences and all the insights I had gained around the issue of power brought me back to taking a closer look at my purpose. With it still being defined as, "manifesting love in the way we do our work in the world", I felt that I was ready to see more. Thankfully the possibility to explore my purpose presented itself quite soon when I was given an opportunity to learn with Tim Kelley.

According to Tim Kelley's true purpose process, purpose is expressed in four aspects: Essence, Blessing, Mission, and Message. During my experience with him, this is what emerged:

My Essence: I am the unity of love and power

My Blessing: to unite love and power

My Mission: to unite love and power on earth

My Message: When love and power are inseparable, humanity will unite

When this emerged, it felt both huge and liberating. It made me understand two things.

1. I could now see why addressing "the manifestation of love" alone was not enough for me anymore.
2. What had been missing in my earlier purpose was power. My soul had been talking to me, through all these intense experiences that I had gone through, and now I could see and understand why.

The dialogue with my Inner Wisdom helped me get out of the overwhelm. The task that I was given in these dialogues was to increase my awareness in my everyday life while holding the question, "how can I take what I have learned and bring it into what is relevant from moment to moment, in everyday life, no matter how small or how big?"

This brought me back in contact with the passionate energy I felt when talking about the power shift and the work we were doing at encode.org. I now looked at it through the lens of my newly discovered purpose. As much as we had been talking about power, I realized I had no idea what we were actually talking about. I became aware of my own assumption that we were all talking about the same thing. How could I assume that, when I wasn't even clear how I defined power for myself?

I began seeking to understand what power actually is, and to explore the meaning personal power has in our lives. What a journey! Some of the greatest thinkers of the world have written on this subject. Plato, Aristotle, Machiavelli, Pareto, Weber, and so many more. Power is a phenomenon talked about and researched in philosophy, psychology, neuroscience, social, and political sciences, and many other fields.

What I found was eye opening on so many levels. I invite you to do an online search for "power meaning". I got about 3.4 billion hits in 0.59 seconds.

Attempting to qualitatively learn and understand, what I found was disconcerting to say the least. One of the more contemporary books on power is Robert Green's *The 48 Laws of Power*. According to Wikipedia this book has sold over 1.2 million copies in the United States alone and has been translated into 24 languages. I started reading it, but just couldn't go through with it. Maybe I missed out on something important, but I found it simply unbearable. It kept bringing back the painful images of my visualizations, the reaction from my own traumas.

Just looking at the table of contents stating the 48 laws was enough to make my body shake and bring the nausea back. It begins with a comparatively mild "law", "never outshine the master". Next is "never put too much trust in friends, learn how to use enemies", which made me gasp. And on it goes: "conceal your intentions", and, "pose as a friend, work as a spy". I couldn't believe it! 48 "laws" telling you how to deceive, lie, and manipulate, all in service of getting you where you want to be. No wonder the New York Magazine review on Amazon says, "Machiavelli has a new rival."

Niccolò Machiavelli was born in 1469 and his book *The Prince* has deeply influenced humanity's stories around power to this day. At its heart is the story that putting your own individual interest above everything else, at the expense of integrity, honesty and relationships, is the best use of power.

In the never-ending string of books and articles that try to define power, most describe power dynamics and how to use those dynamics to gain "power over". At a minimum, this looks like gaining a competitive advantage on the path up the career ladder. Apart from examples like Robert Green's book, few of these texts are rooted in a mindset of ruthless self-interest. Nonetheless, many confirm that at the end of the day someone needs to hold ultimate power.

Some of what's written is clearly well-intentioned and suggests that power can support more effective service in the world. This is perhaps best summed up by Baltasar Gracián, a Spanish Jesuit and baroque prose writer and philosopher born in the early 1600s. He said, "the sole advantage of power is that you can do more good". I believe this sentiment is at the core of most purpose-guided and mission-driven entities, for-profit and nonprofit businesses alike, and the fairly new field of "Social Business". In one way or the other, these endeavors tend to be about gaining power to improve one or more local, communal, societal, or global phenomena which are seen as unsatisfactory, lacking, unjust, or otherwise harmful. Ultimately, this means gaining power over something so that it can be changed.

In the end, even when based on the best of intentions, the story is always about success through power over. We can find the underlying story, that we must have power over something in order to change it, reflected in absolutely all aspects of our life—individually, and in the systems in which we are embedded. Even when we talk about "power with"—about collaboration, co-creation, distribution, and decentralization—the most practical manifestations don't go through with it. Just to name two examples, this "power with" energy shows up as distributed or self-managed teams, but those teams are still embedded in a management hierarchy and/or have a team leader. Or we implement a system with distributed authority which doesn't address personal power, because power and authority are conflated and seen as one[15].

---

[15] Further reading: Blog post at https://christianesplace.com/blog/is-distributed-power-a-myth

Speaking of conflation, power is very often addressed in connection with leadership, possibly based on the assumption that without "power over" there is no leadership. Though this sounds true, it always created a sense of unease for me, which led me to write an article called "Leadership and Power Shift—The Unconscious Dichotomy that is Holding us Back"[16].

Concepts like "Servant Leadership", "Evolutionary Leadership", and "Conscious Leadership" have had an important, positive impact by helping shift the image of a leader away from the "Heroic Leader", showing up as force, leading with "power over". Even with these evolving concepts, there's still an underlying story that a) being a leader is not for everyone, and b) if you are a leader, you need to develop a number of traits, qualities, and skills that will make you even better—ideally great. "Once you are a great leader, others will follow you" is a story that just doesn't sit right with me.

The exact same feeling of discomfort is triggered in me when I hear, "we have bad leadership". Pointing at the people who are "the leaders" reveals an underlying dynamic that separates *those who are leaders* from *those who are not*. I just can't buy into these stories because I believe that the underlying issue really is power—how people use power, and how easily leadership, including the connected power, is handed off to others.

At one point I had to accept that I was getting nowhere. I was looking for something, but I didn't know what it was. All I knew was that almost every time I learned something new about power or found a new perspective on what power is and how it plays out in our lives, I felt this sense of unease and restlessness. I felt this desire to escape, combined with a feeling of paralysis. I realized that confronting the issue of power triggered trauma in my nervous system.

Once again, adding perspective helped me to move on. I found an additional perspective in a new aspect of my inner child. Caroline

---

[16] Further reading: Blog post at https://christianesplace.com/blog/leadership-and-power-shift

Myss would call it the "Wounded Child", who "holds the memories of abuse, neglect and other traumas that we have endured during childhood"[17]. In dialogue with this part of me, I could see that I was holding a "when/then" energy in connection with my learnings and my quest. My unconscious pattern was built on a story, "when I have resolved the trauma that keeps paralyzing me, then I will be able to continue my search." What kept me running in circles was the feeling that there was something wrong with me that needed to be fixed, and my expectation towards myself to fix it. My "Wounded Child" made me see that, for where I was in my life at this moment, it was enough to acknowledge this child part of me. Seeing its connection to the trauma that I was holding, and seeing the potential for healing through this, was enough. I could trust that I was where I was supposed to be, that healing would come whenever the time was right, and that there was nothing I needed to wait for.

As I returned to the question of how I could bring my learnings into my everyday life, Adam Kahane's book *Power and Love: A Theory and Practice of Social Change* found me. It was published in 2009 and I discovered it eight or nine years later. I was amazed—actually, shocked—to find that with all the learning I had done on power, this book never showed up in my search. But, here it was, and thus my journey could continue.

I read the book in one day and night and then read it again to take notes. I will forever be grateful to Adam Kahane for the incredible work he has done and still is doing. His book brought everything to me that I needed at that point to continue manifesting my purpose. From Martin Luther King, Jr.'s writings, to Dr. King's doctoral advisor Paul Tillich, to Jungian psychologist Robert Johnson, and many others, to which Mr. Kahane points to in his book, filled many gaps for me and opened the pathway that led, eventually, to my writing this book.

---

[17] You can find great free resources on Caroline Myss' Website here: https://www.myss.com/free-resources/sacred-contracts-and-your-archetypes/appendix-the-four-archetypes-of-survival/

When I finished my first reading of *Power and Love*, I became aware of an inner conflict that I had completely suppressed. While on my quest around power I had been shutting down an inner voice asking, "what about love?". I had not been able to see the connection between love and power in a way that felt aligned with my purpose. It was as though I had been afraid of misunderstanding or finding the wrong way to embody the unification of love and power.

Thanks in large part to Paul Tillich's definitions of love and power, the dots slowly connected. Finally, I had found a definition of power that, in the way I understood it, represented it as a natural phenomenon, something that simply *is*. For the first time in my life, power felt like something that could actually give rise to a new story: one that holds the potential to support the healing of the innumerable—past and ongoing, individual and collective—traumas caused by the old story of "power over".

Paul Tillich says, "power is the drive of everything living to realize itself, with increasing intensity and extensity[18]."

With this understanding, everything began to connect and make sense in a whole new way for me.

We are all here for a reason

Continuing with the perspective that spirit, consciousness, and nature are three different words to describe the infinite realm of all being and becoming, and that our soul is a finite location within the infinite realm, we can see that each of us has unique potential to contribute to the greater whole. Us being here in this life is spirit's offering to us, to explore and manifest that potential.

Power is our drive to do this work, to self-realize our soul potential, with increasing intensity and extensity— to become ever

---

[18] Collins English Dictionary: extensity - the quality of having extension; that quality of sensation which permits the perception of space or size

more of who we truly are. Power is what we have, individually and collectively, and we ultimately have a choice in how we use it. All this leads to a new story about power—one where power is an ever-present phenomenon, based in spirit-consciousness-nature.

Marilyn Hamilton, Founder of Integral City[19], put it beautifully in one of the many inspiring articles[20] on her blog. "'Power Over' is dominator based. 'Power With' is relationship-based. 'Power As' is consciousness based." She goes on, "Power As is called forth because Power With seems powerless against Power Over. Power With has the best intentions to include Power Over in the dialogues and collaborations it imagines and attempts. But Power With fails to recognize the capacity for hijacking resources that Power Over can too easily manipulate. Only Power As is willing to speak Truth to Power Over and offer Appropriate Love (and not be naively manipulated) to Power With. Power As has the wisdom to act AS Life to realign and recalibrate the inappropriate use of the Powers that have evolved in earlier eras."

The way my new story of power had emerged and shaped filled me with great joy, hope, and passion.

Power is the gift of spirit-consciousness-nature that enables the manifestation of purpose, thus to be of service to the interconnected and interdependent greater whole.

I wrote this on a piece of paper, decorated it so it became a colorful picture, and put it on my laptop as my screen background. Every time I saw it, my heartbeat faster. I always felt the same joy, hope, and passion. As excited and inspired as I was by the new story of power that had emerged for me, I was aware that I still had a way to go to understand my purpose. I hadn't yet found what *the unification of love and power* meant, and how I could manifest it in my life.

---

[19] https://integralcity.com/
[20] https://integralcity.com/2020/03/21/organizational-power-power-over-power-with-power-as/

By now I was fully aware that my journey of dealing with purpose, power, and love meant dealing with my own story, and my own relationship to these three phenomena. My exploration of the story of purpose and power had been very intense, and even painful. In the end, the journey was liberating, joyful, inspiring, humbling, and gratifying. Embarking on an exploration of the story of love, I assumed the journey would be no different.

The story of love

At the time when my purpose, as best I knew, was, "the manifestation of love in the way we do our work in the world", I had actually never asked myself what love meant to me. I have to smile at myself now, in retrospect. Back then, I was content with my general sense that love is a strong emotional connection, at play when we can say, "I love you", or, "I love it", and really mean it.

Now, guided by my new purpose, I felt a need for much more clarity. In finding Adam Kahane's book and with it Paul Tillich's definitions of power and of love, I had found a very good starting point for a new exploratory journey. My guiding question was, "what is the story of love that holds the potential to support the manifestation of unified love and power in service to purpose?"

I began collecting material to read, watch, or listen to. Soon my research list became overbearing. From the ancient Greek to contemporary philosophers by the hundreds, be they Eastern, Western, and indigenous, to practically all religious writings, innumerable non-fiction books, novels, poetry, songs, and movies—I came to believe that love is the most widely addressed issue in the world.

Researching love was like traveling through time and space. Every time I read, watched, or listened to something, I learned about similarities and differences and heard something new. I could absorb it all almost completely without any filters of judgment. I found these perspectives incredibly inspiring. I remembered how judgmental I had felt about the book *48 Laws of Power* and other works on that topic, but with love it was different. Almost everything I found was uplifting, inspiring, and wonderful.

Nonetheless, I began to develop a strange feeling that what I was doing wasn't helping me. I decided to reconnect to the excitement I had felt when reading Paul Tillich's definition:

"Love is the drive to unify the separated, not to create unity, but to reveal the unity that is there."

Over months I sat in contemplation with this definition. The longer I tried to fully understand the meaning of it, the more I felt that rather than giving me an answer, it was inviting me into something.

Once again grateful for my JournaLogue practice, I went into introspection through dialogue with my inner parts. Until then I had been in dialogue with my Inner Wisdom and a number of other parts of myself. It had not yet occurred to me to connect to and communicate directly with the part in me that is my Power. Now, when I began to search for a deeper understanding of love, my Inner Wisdom suggested I invite both my Love and my Power into dialogue, beginning with my Power.

Even though I had dealt with the issue of power so intensively, it seemed that in order to begin my exploration about love, I needed to build my relationship with my own Power through direct dialogue. In this moment, I got a first glimpse of how the two—love and power—really never are separate, but I had a long journey ahead of me before I could fully embrace and integrate this understanding.

When I addressed my Power—the part of "Power As" that is my unique and authentic power to self-realize—it invited me to explore what it means to embody this authentic power in my everyday life. This question immediately gave rise to a sense of fear. This was confirmed later by participants in my research about authentic power, many of whom experienced a similar response.

At first I resisted this fear. I was disappointed with myself. After all the wonderful insights I had had about power, why did it still feel scary to act from and with it? The fear was telling me something, however, and I knew that I wouldn't be able to move on in my quest without understanding it.

Two things emerged through the voice of my Power that helped me move on at this point:

"True power emerges from unity. When there is no unity, there is no power—there is only force."

And, "you need to know that when you embody your true authentic power, you are always acting from love at the same time. As long as you are not aware that love is inseparable from power in general, and that your authentic love is inseparable from your authentic power, you will be afraid of embodying it."

Here it was again—the word "unity", like in the definition of love: "… reveal the unity that is there". Being unaware of this unity creates the potential for one, or both, of two things: force and fear.

Seeing "force" come up again brought me back to the assumption that the mutual root cause of all traumas is "power over", being wielded forcefully. It seems we humans are capable of unbelievable atrocities when we powerfully self-realize while *disconnected* from love. This disconnect enables us to force our individual or our collective needs, our ways, our beliefs, our culture, our physical strength, our sex drive, and so much more on others who have less power. We know from many examples throughout human history that where people wield power forcefully over others, they generally believe that what they are doing serves something that is right and good despite the often catastrophic evidence of harm.

So many questions came up for me. Can it be that we have learned to develop stories of legitimization—stories through which we then feel legitimized to self-realize forcefully, over others? If our authentic power is inseparable from love, can it be that these stories of legitimization are what enable us to disconnect from love? By developing these stories of legitimization, do we actually make an extra effort to move love out of the way, so to speak, so we can yield "power over" forcefully? And once we believe these stories of legitimization and disconnect from love, does that prevent us from being aware of what we are actually here to self-realize—our purpose?

> "Power without love is reckless and abusive, and love without power is sentimental and anemic."
> —Dr. Martin Luther King, Jr.

Though challenged by these many questions, I knew I needed to hold them and let them accompany me on my quest. I still needed to learn about my own fear first.

What was I afraid of? Acting from my authentic power meant manifesting my purpose, so why did that create this fear that was holding me back? I remembered the part of my journey where I became aware of cutting myself off from my feelings—the disturbing image of a guillotine—and the roots of this fearful pattern. I thought that removing the block between my body and mind had resolved my issues around feeling heard, seen, and acknowledged for who I truly am, but I now saw more was needed.

"Don't be ridiculous"

In the process of building my relationship with my authentic power through direct inner dialogue, Power asked me to invite my Creativity to join the conversation. As a reminder, my Creativity is what emerged from my Wounded Child. When I asked to invite my Love into the conversation as well, both Power and Creativity told me that it was too early for that.

Creativity led me back into a childhood memory. It was a memory I had never quite forgotten, and I now remembered that it had popped up repeatedly over time. Every time I had discarded it, pushed it away, and shut my ears to its call to learn from what it was telling me. Supported by my Power and Creativity, the time was now right to look at this memory and the whole experience came back to me in full clarity.

I must have been about six or seven years old. We lived in a big house, divided into three sections: one section for my family, one section for my father's sister and her family, and one for my father's brother and his family. A girl cousin, a little younger than I, told me that she had begun ballet classes. Though we had never been very close, I was fascinated and wanted her to show me what she learned. From then on we met regularly in our yard, where she showed me what she was learning. We danced together, without music but with a lot of joy. Eventually she invited me over to her place and loaned me one of her ballet outfits (which, admittedly, was quite a bit too small) . We started rehearsing a performance for my grandparents, whose impending visit had been announced to us. When indoors, we were able to dance to the music from *Swan Lake*.

Being a parent and an aunt myself, today I know what it means to sit through children's home performances. They are always delivered with so much joy and enthusiasm but can be a bit hard to sit through with a straight face and the required appreciation. Today I have to smile when I imagine the scene in my uncle's living room. Two little girls taking turns, hopping out from behind a drawn curtain, proudly performing their impression of Swan Lake. I remember the enthusiasm and the joy of moving to the music that I felt at the time, while performing what I thought was ballet in my too-small outfit.

Shortly after this performance I approached my father and told him that I would love to take ballet lessons. His reaction was mortifying. He burst out laughing and said, "you? Ballet lessons? Don't be ridiculous! No, forget it. You are not getting ballet lessons."

I was stunned. It wasn't the "no" that hurt the most. It was the laughter, the word "ridiculous". In my head I saw myself doing the performance, thinking I was performing something nice, and how this memory shattered inside of me. I was ridiculous. With a last little straw of hope I went to my mother, hoping that maybe she would help me. I was up for another strike. Like my father, my mother laughed out loud and said the exact same words: "don't be ridiculous".

I remember feeling as if I'd been thrown into ice water. As is typical for a child, I didn't question my parents' judgment, but believed them. I remembered how I had felt when moving my body to music, allowing the sound to flow through my body and letting my body react and freely express itself. Today, I know that this time when I was dancing with my cousin was the only time in my childhood where I could feel fully like myself—like "me". What I made from the experience with my parents was that this "me" was ridiculous.

I know now that from then on I developed an incredible capacity to be what I believed others would want me to be. I wouldn't be ridiculous. I learned to trade being "me" for being "what was expected of me." Life for me, quite unconsciously, became about being what others would see as "good". If I couldn't do that, I wouldn't be loved. In the worst case, I would be abandoned.

As my self-reflection practice took me through this memory, it felt as if it had happened only yesterday. It brought up all the pain I had not allowed to emerge at the time. I cried for days, just letting it flow, encouraged by my Power and Creativity to let it all come out. Eventually the tears dried up and at the same time I felt a sense of gratitude that my psyche had not allowed me to feel all this pain as a child. I imagine it would have been close to unbearable then.

Isn't it wonderful how, as children, we have all these survival mechanisms that help us form patterns to deal with pain—and then, later on in our life, we are offered choices to learn about our patterns and to resolve and transform those that we decide we want to change?

Up to that time I had done many years of therapy, done shadow work, and learned many different ways to get to know and understand myself better. I combined many of these learnings in my JournaLogue methodology for self-coaching. Only now, after having gone all the way into this pain, was I ready to move on. This took seeing it, feeling it again, then letting it go and feeling gratitude for how as a child I had been able to guard myself from larger pain.

Knowing how trauma plays out in general and how it had played out for my parents enabled me to see my childhood experiences without blaming and shaming. I don't know why my parents were so completely unaware of what was going on for me in the story about my wish for ballet lessons, but I'm sure that in this and other hurtful circumstances their intention was to do what was best and right. They could only see this through their set of values and beliefs, and only act from the possibilities they had available at that point in time—influenced by their own life and their own traumas.

Another aspect that became clear to me emerged from my memory of how wonderful my body had felt when I was dancing. When told, "don't be ridiculous!" by both my parents, I translated that not only into, "I am ridiculous", but, "my body is ridiculous when expressing myself freely." I could see now that there were many things I would have loved to do as a child, and even as an adult, that would have involved bodily expression. I didn't do them because of the completely unconscious story I was holding: my body was ridiculous.

Looking deeper, I saw that I would never be able to *embody* my authentic power, thus manifest my purpose, without fully including my body.

This was the moment I understood why I had been so drawn to Arawana Hayashi's[21] work of "Embodied Presence". I met Arawana at a Theory U Foundation Course of the Presencing Institute[22]. As much as I appreciate Otto Scharmer's Theory U work, what reached me the most was the embodiment work Arawana offered. It seems that my soul was whispering to me, nudging me into this opportunity for connection to my body. This

---

[21] Find more about Arawana's work here: https://arawanahayashi.com
[22] Find detailed information here: https://www.presencing.org

connection had been completely missing in my life. After all, I considered it to be ridiculous!

After I had reflected on my childhood experience around the ballet lessons, I also understood why, up until that point, I had never gotten comfortable when going through the exercises in Arawana's programs: I was not well connected to my body and could not understand its language.

Determined to reinhabit my own body more fully, I signed up for Arawana's one year "Social Presencing Theater Advanced" (SPT) course. I was eager to heal my relationship with my body and learn to understand its language. I knew this was missing in all aspects of my life. The SPT Advanced course was a beautiful learning experience for me. At times, because of old patterns coming back, it was quite difficult. SPT helped me in building a completely new relationship with my body, and to begin to integrate the vast source of information it holds for me in all aspects of my life. The program also opened me up to seeing the deeper meaning that embodiment can have on a collective level. There are no words sufficient to express the gratitude and appreciation I have for Arawana and her work.

Only now could I develop a sense of the unity of body, mind, heart, and spirit. I experience mindfulness—being present in the moment, sensing into and being available for what wants to emerge—with a completely new quality when I am open to emergence on all these four levels. When closing off any one of them, something essential is missing. Consciously practicing the integration of all four levels as I navigated my daily life gave me an understanding of Wholeness. To me Wholeness, on a personal level, is the unity of body, mind, heart, and spirit. I don't need to "become" whole—I am whole, at any given moment, through this unity.

Building a new relationship with my body after a life of judgment and disconnection wasn't easy. It is an ongoing journey, and exploration of what lies in my shadow. My own judgments and disconnection had been influenced and amplified by the overarching and omni-present themes in our society of how a body "should" look, and how we "should" be.

Discovering your own unique beauty

This story of "shoulds" drives one of the biggest industries in the world, the wellness and fitness industry. Insecurities and judgements about our bodies serve this industry and its ongoing deceiving promises of "when/then". When you are (fill in the blank), then you'll be happy. Fill in the blank with thinner, prettier, fitter, younger-looking, more successful, richer, higher-status, in a relationship, loved, etc. It has become completely normal to run continuously after what we don't yet have. This creates an ongoing sense of scarcity, of not having, of missing out. This completely disconnects us from the unique beauty of each and every one of us, just as we are, and our personal sense of why we are here.

As long as we are disconnected from the unique beauty that we are, we are incapable of embodying our authentic power—because our authentic power lies in this uniqueness.

We learn to see our unique beauty through building a conscious relationship with our body, mind, heart, and spirit. For me, the relationship to my body had been deeply damaged. For others, their obstacles might lie somewhere else. Some might think they are not intelligent enough, or not capable of true loving connections, or doubt their soul and have no real sense of meaning in their life. No matter how they manifest, I believe that all these feelings of inadequacy, of something missing, of scarcity, are stories that develop early in our lives. These stories are layered over our unique beauty, our authentic being, and they prevent us from seeing our essence. These layers are waiting to be peeled off, one by one, during our own personal journey of learning and expressing ever more of who we truly are.

Fully embodying my authentic power would mean showing myself fully, on all levels—and herein lay the fear. As long as I hadn't begun healing my relationship with my body, I wasn't brave enough to be seen.

Embodying our authentic power means showing ourselves as fully as we can at any given moment in time. When this triggers fear, we can see it as a pointer towards a healing opportunity on the levels of body, mind, heart, and spirit.

"Healing" myself means becoming aware of disconnection and consciously building connection to myself on all levels. The unity of body, mind, heart, and spirit is the "channel" for love flowing through us—for self-love.

At the beginning of my quest to better understand love, I needed to take this detour back into deepening my understanding of authentic power. My authentic power is the part of universal power, of Power As, that is within me. It is my personal part of that natural, flowing phenomenon that is as it is. Through "Authentic Power As", I can learn ever more of who I truly am, self-realize, and manifest my purpose.

Authentic power can only be embodied when it is united with authentic love—with self-love.

With this insight the time felt right for me to integrate my love into my daily JournaLogue practice. As always, to begin such an inner dialogue I needed to build the relationship with this part. I thought I was ready, but it was surprisingly difficult. My understanding of love was still vague, and I even had the idea that the part in me that *is* love was just as vague.

I went back to Paul Tillich's definition of love— "the drive to unify the separated, not to create unity, but to reveal the unity that is there." Something about this definition was equally intriguing and confusing to me. What confused me was, "the drive to unify the separated". The part that intrigued me and that created a sense of strong resonance was, "to reveal the unity that is there".

I returned to exploring how I was currently defining love. Prior to being driven by my purpose to understand it better, I had seen love as an emotion, triggered by a sense of meaningful connection between people, between people and animals, or toward other things in the world. It could be expressed in ways like, "I love you", or "I love being in nature". One could love a pet, animals in general, music, or any of a number of other things. And then there was the other side: disliking a person meant, for me, not to love them. One could dislike being in nature in the rain or cold, which meant not loving nature under these circumstances, or dislike an animal such as a rat or a spider. Love for me had been reserved for what I considered worthy: living up to specific, often unconscious criteria.

At first I didn't like what this taught me about myself. Obviously, I was holding love as something that could only be experienced and expressed when certain conditions were met. I was aware there was something like unconditional love, and being a mother, I certainly knew that this was the love I felt for my son. Only in connection with my son had I sensed my love being completely and absolutely unquestionable, under any circumstances. Otherwise, when it came to trying to understand love in general, I kept seeing this difference between the unconditional love I felt for my son and the "other" love: love for the "worthy" and therefore "lovable" people or things.

Cognitively I knew that something was wrong with this. Being honest with myself, I knew that this sense of "something is wrong" was calling for my attention. From somewhere inside of me I kept hearing a voice telling me, "you can't love everything!", or "think of person X and all the terrible things this person has done. You can't love X!", or "look what company Y is doing to our environment. There's nothing lovable about Y!".

I reread my journal from the point when I consciously started my quest around love. What stuck out for me were the phrases, "the unique beauty that we are" and "self-love". It dawned on me that the way I was holding love didn't just apply to the world around me—it also applied to myself. Despite everything I had learned about self-love, deep down in my shadow, I was still holding on to the belief that I too needed to prove that I was worthy of being loved, both by others and by myself. I had much more to learn about loving myself before I could move on.

In the JournaLogue session where this came up, I heard an inner voice saying loud and clear, "you are not worthy of unconditional love". As in prior experiences, my body reacted immediately. First, I got so cold that I shivered, and then I started to sweat. At the same time, I was in tears. On the one hand, I desperately wanted to do something to stop this terrible feeling. On the other, I knew that this was what needed to happen, what held the potential to help me move on. Only by moving through this experience could I connect with what lay beyond, and what wanted to be seen.

I knew this voice came from my shadow, so I began to visualize myself with a torch walking toward what looked like a cave. Though really frightened, I willed myself to enter the cave. As I did, the entire scene changed. I was back at my childhood home, perhaps four or five years old. I entered our yard through a huge green iron gate. As it always had been, it was difficult for me to open. I could hear the voices of my two cousins further down in the yard. They were approximately my age, and I decided to join them to play.

They were not alone. With them was their Nanny, an elderly woman who had been with the family for decades. In fact, she'd been the Nanny of my father and his siblings. She had never been particularly fond of my sisters and me, as we tended to be more on the rough side when playing—more often playing pirates or cowboys than playing with dolls. I imagine she felt she needed to be protective of her little charges.

As I walked towards my cousins, she looked at me, sighed, and said, "oh dear—not you again!" I was confused and asked her why she didn't want me to be there with my cousins. She told me that I was a naughty child, always up to something forbidden. In her eyes, I remembered, climbing a tree was already forbidden because it was too risky. I always loved climbing trees and sitting up there, high in the sky.

And then she continued. "Well, you always behave like a naughty boy, which is no wonder. When you were born your mother had a hysterical crying fit when she saw that you were another girl!"

At that point in my vision, the picture froze, and I had an out of body experience. A part of me left my child body, flew up into the air, and looked down at little Christiane. I saw her face—stunned, completely motionless, staring at Nanny. I knew she was completely numb, because I was the one holding a terrible, almost unbearable, piercing pain. Looking down on little Christiane, I was so glad she couldn't feel this pain. I knew it would have been too much for her. After a short while I—the separated part of little Christiane—sank down again, just before my body merged back into hers, I crouched, and something folded all around me.

I was now looking at the Nanny again, but I felt different than before. I felt heavier, and weirdly old in my child body. In my mind I wanted to turn around and skip away, but my body didn't do that. It was too heavy. I could only move in slow motion, so I turned and very slowly walked back from whence I came.

As I—little Christiane—walked out through the iron gate, my awareness returned to the present moment. I was sitting in my usual spot, where I always do my journaling practice. I turned my awareness inward to my Love and asked it for help. Now Love was fully available for our dialogue. It reached out and embraced me in the most wonderful way. I asked it to help me find that part of me that I had experienced, separating from little Christiane and holding the pain. Love helped me, and the part eventually showed up in the form of a cuddled up, very small body—a sleeping child, in the center of a water lily, leaves folded over the child in protection. This vision came at the beginning of a wonderful, healing process about self-love that is still going on today.

Only what you love can heal

I will never know, and don't need to know, if what Nanny told me was true or not. I know that the pain of the memory coming out of the shadow was an expression of the trauma my body had been holding, and that the inner process of separation from that pain was vital to me as a child. It was my survival mechanism at the time. As I had before, I felt gratitude for this inner process of self-protection. This opened up an enormous possibility for healing. I needed this experience of facing a pain that was stored in my body before I could really connect to my Love.

When it came to self-love, I felt that this memory tied to the deepest root that I needed to explore. Looking back at my life, I could see how many of my experiences and resulting behaviors were influenced by the deep root of my trauma. Many things began to make sense.

I had an experience like sitting in a dark room and, one after the other, watching spotlights click on—each shining their light on a picture, showing a specific moment in my life where my thought and behavior patterns were grounded in stories like, "I am not wanted as who I am. I need to be something different. I need to be what others want me to be, so they accept and love me. When they accept and love me, I can accept and love myself."

Each of these images showed not what had actually happened, but what I had made of them—and I'd piled them up, one upon the other, to form my belief patterns. Each now offered me a healing opportunity. At this time, I received a wonderfully helpful message from my Love.

"I hold the space for your healing. Only what you love can heal."

Each spot lit memory related to how I perceived others judging me, disregarding me, or otherwise leaving me feeling unappreciated. I could see how this made me unconsciously adapt my behavior in order to shift the situation in pursuit of the appreciation, acknowledgment, and love that I craved. In retrospect, I could see how over time my behavior became ever less authentic, and how this confused others and increased the disconnect.

I kept holding the sentence, "only what you love can heal." As I learned to see each of these memories as a learning opportunity, I learned to love even these experiences now that I was ready to receive their lessons. I was grateful for the choice to see my history from a different perspective.

Reflecting on one memory after the other, I had the most astounding insight. When bringing the memories up in retrospect, I could feel the pain—but remembering how I had experienced the moments in my past, I noticed many of them hadn't felt painful at the time. I had "translated" pain into something else, leaning into the survival pattern of behaving in a certain way, unconsciously refusing to experience pain. I accepted these experiences as "normal". This pattern repeated itself until I was older, ready to face the pain and to learn from it.

Now that I was aware of my past pain and ready to face it, reflect on it, learn from it, and transform it, I expected healing. As it so often goes with specific expectations, I soon found out that I was set up for disappointment. I thought that facing the pain and seeing its root cause would make it go away, but it didn't. I had to look at the story I was holding around what "healing" meant. Healing went deeper than I'd realized and involved resolving *everything* that was in the way of living through the unity of body, heart, mind, and spirit. I had more work ahead before my childhood traumas and old survival strategies could be resolved and integrated into my being.

Unlike physical injuries (cuts) or illnesses (pneumonia), my painful memories didn't resolve with "treatment"—with treatment, in this case, being reflection and forgiveness rather than bandages and antibiotics. My memories started showing up in dreams—sometimes very unpleasant ones. I felt restless and tired, and my disappointment—mostly with myself—grew. Though I remembered what my Love had told me: "only what you love can heal"—I couldn't ground in the self-love that was needed.

It was a conversation with my Inner Wisdom that helped me move forward. It invited me to repeat after it: "I am uniquely beautiful, and I love who I am."

It invited me to keep repeating this over and over again, and after every repetition I had to say how it felt to speak this out. My answers—"I can't feel it," or, "It just doesn't really sink in," spoke to the inner barriers I'd built against self-acceptance. After many repetitions, in my visualization, my Love came to sit beside me and held me in her arms. That's when something inside me cracked open. From somewhere in the shadows, I could suddenly hear what was holding me back from fully believing my words.

What I heard was an angry voice, shouting, "this is so bad! You are arrogant and vain!" And then, even louder, "it is not for you to say!"

Those were the stories I had been holding and that were sabotaging me. I saw these beliefs, and how completely unquestioned they'd been for all my life. To think of myself as beautiful, let alone speak it out, was bad, arrogant, and vain. What felt the biggest was, "it is not for me to say". This story had made me completely dependent on judgment from outside. This disconnection from myself stood in the way of my self-love.

This experience was the beginning of a new relationship with an inner part of myself called "M". M is short for "Moralizer", which was the name in the beginning. After a while the part didn't like to be called that any more and asked me to shorten its name. Through M, among many other things, I learned a deeper understanding of healing. There was no way I could ask anything to simply go away. I needed to accept and embrace it.

Together we explored how I had never given M any attention at first—I had kept it rigidly in its place, with stories about it sabotaging my efforts at accepting myself. In our conversations I learned so much about myself, and M has completely transformed. It is now a very important member of my "Inner Support Team". M has shifted to be the voice of integrity and authenticity and when I am not quite sure about a decision, M's perspective is invaluable for me to see what the best next step might be.

Healing doesn't mean that what once hurt us goes away. Like a scar on a cut finger, what was hurt may bear a mark. The scar isn't the pain, though. It's a reminder of what happened once upon a time, and once it's integrated it becomes a part of us.

"You can only heal what you love".

It's about accepting the scar, not holding on to the pain. Healing means connecting and accepting. Healing means loving.

Shifting from a belief that, "I am not wanted as who I am" to believing, "I love myself unconditionally as who I am" is a beautiful, often very difficult, and always transformational journey of healing trauma. For me, finding a new story of love required addressing trauma, as had finding a new story of power.

In my work around love, another one of my old patterns was still showing up. It was the "when/then" pattern. I discovered that I was now driven by the conviction that only when I loved myself unconditionally would I be able to self-realize and manifest my purpose. My thoughts unsettled me, telling me there was so much of myself to explore, learn, and heal. "I'll never get to the point where I can love myself unconditionally," I thought. "I'll probably never be able to step into my authentic power and manifest my purpose!"

Reliably, my Love offered me words that helped me overcome this sense of overwhelm.

"Self-love is a process, not a state. Self-love means turning from judgment to curiosity."

This is when I remembered Byron Katie's work on "Loving What Is". In connection with my ongoing learning, I took this to mean that self-love is about being present with what is and loving it.

When we are present with what is, awareness replaces judgment.

Grounded in this awareness, we can explore with a "beginner's mind"—open, curious, and without preconceptions. Loving ourselves unconditionally is an ongoing process, not a state. It is the process of learning ever more of who we are.

We are a unique piece of art at any given moment in time, and continuously in the making. We are perfect as we are, from moment to moment.

Self-love has no beginning and no end. It rests and it moves. It is an inseparable part of Love As. It is where love is anchored within us. It is in us, it flows through us, it *is* us—an inseparable part of everything.

This new way of understanding self-love enabled me to open up to my traumas and shadows and learn from them in a whole new way—most importantly, without suffering from them anymore. Sure, I still fall back into old patterns, but now I can see each of those occurrences as a creative tension: a tension that, through being addressed, will reveal just a bit more of the piece of art that I am. I do this on an ongoing basis in my daily JournaLogue practice, which often includes embodied presence practices; through drawing; or sometimes even through humming or singing. Every once in a while, I still get stuck—and then I seek help from a friend, a book or media, a coach, or a therapist.

From my own experience, I can say that suffering from the difficult things that happened to us in our lives is what points us towards the opportunity to heal. Healing means connecting what was disconnected. While we cannot make our painful experiences go away or pretend they never happened, we can see them simply as part of our life that brought us to where we are today. They are part of us, part of our unique beauty.

I recently watched the documentary "The Wisdom of Trauma" produced and published by Science and Nonduality (SAND). So much in the film resonated with my experiences. In the film, Dr. Gabor Maté says, "underneath that traumatized persona, there is the healthy individual, who has never found expression in this life.

If you see that, then you are trauma informed. It's not a question of healing the trauma or getting rid of the memory of what happened, but to help that person expand and give space for all those emotions." This was exactly what I had experienced on my journey, both through the exploration of power and the exploration of love.

As I continued my quest to understand and manifest my purpose, I turned to my Love again. Here's an excerpt from my JournaLogue practice:

> Me: Even after all I have learned from you, I still feel quite overwhelmed at times to connect to you and to talk to you. You seem so . . . big, so . . . endless.
>
> *Love: Try and imagine different forms through which I express myself: through self, through other, and through all.*
>
> *"Love through self" means loving yourself, which you have thoroughly explored. "Love through other" means loving everything in the entire, more-than-human world.*
>
> *"Love through all" means loving all that is, through surrendering to the unknown. It is this "love through all" that enables you to integrate what it means that everything is connected—everything known and unknown. It includes surrendering to the unknown.*
>
> *None of these three expressions of love are possible on their own. Love is always whole—Love As.*
>
> *Love is also a sentiment, an emotion that we feel. It is also so much more. The journey your life is offering you is to learn how to grow to love ever more of everything, because you are connected to everything, thus everything is connected to you. Love is the connection of everything with everything.*
>
> Me: It seems that the love we feel as emotion is a part of Love As. It seems to be the easier part for us, because through being aware of it we can deal with it.

Love As is the connectedness of everything. The parts of it that we are not consciously aware of, or that we feel separated from, are there nonetheless and are waiting—wanting—to be seen. We can see them when we search for them, and shine light onto them through our reflection and introspection. Ah, now I understand! When we allow connection to reveal itself to us, then we can feel it in the form of love as emotion. We experience ourselves as "in love". When the connectedness of everything reveals itself to us, we can love—and can be in love with—everything. We might always find things that challenge us and that we cannot understand or identify with, but once the connectedness of everything—Love As—has entered our awareness as a foundational pattern of being, we have the choice to understand that everything is there for a reason.

Charles Eisenstein writes in his book *The Ascent of Humanity*[23], "if our ruinous civilization is built on a struggle of good versus evil, then its healing demands the opposite: self-acceptance, self-love, and self-trust. Contrary to our best intentions, we will never end the evil and violence of our civilization by trying harder to overcome, regulate, and control a human nature we deem evil, for the war on human nature, no less than the war on nature, generates only more separation, more violence, more hatred. 'You can kill the haters,' said Martin Luther King, 'but you cannot kill the hate.' The master's tools will never dismantle the master's house. The same applies internally. You can go to war against parts of yourself you think are bad, but even if you win, like the Bolsheviks and the Maoists, the victors become the new villains. The separation from self that the campaign of willpower entails cannot but be projected, eventually, in some form, onto the outside world."

For me, and perhaps for you as well, the biggest challenge is to surrender to Love As so that I can see how everything—even those things I despise and that cause me pain—are a part of (inter) being and are there for a reason. I repeatedly encounter situations

---

[23] https://ascentofhumanity.com/text/

where I feel judgment arise, where I feel something is bad and I feel compelled to prove that it is wrong or even fight against it. Sometimes I feel something bad or evil is being done to me, to other living beings, or to the planet. When these situations show up, I can now see them as yet another invitation to love.

Thankfully there are many practices that can support us to shift out of the blame game, which holds so much toxic energy, and into mindful presence. With the JournaLogue, I have found my own practice for processing these experiences, holding the intention to explore how I can shift from judgment to curiosity and the perspective of Love As. It helps me to step back into the experience of the connectedness of everything, to surrender to what is, and to make my choices from there.

Sometimes, when I am having a hard time, I go back and read a dialogue I had with my Love.

Me: How do I know I love enough?

Love: "Enough" implies that Love could be finite. Love is infinite. Take a deep breath and repeat to yourself: Love is infinite.

Me: That's wonderful. And now I am aware of a self-doubt that's coming up. It feels like I still need to resolve something before my love is good enough.

Love: It is not the level of love that makes it "good" or "bad". Love doesn't exist in those dimensions. What changes is your awareness about its presence. It is ok to be distracted. What can help is to develop a "love sensor". This sensor can give you a signal when you are moving towards a state of disconnect. In everyday life, when we are calm and peacefully going about our life, we don't need to keep "thinking" of love. We can trust that we are always connected through love anyway. It is impossible to not be connected. But what we sometimes do is to construct a disconnect in our thoughts. Those thoughts then give rise to various emotions like anxiety, fear, anger, and disappointment, and can lead us to blaming and shaming. All these emotions are wonderful signals that call for our attention and awareness. When we can attune our "sensor" to them and turn toward these emotions with curiosity, we can then ask questions like, "what is going on with me right now?", "what is revealing itself to me?", and "what can I learn about myself through this?". These questions bring us back into awareness of our interdependence and interconnectedness.

Everything is part of the web of life, and it is love that connects the parts of this web—self, other, and all. To love other or all means to love ourselves. To love ourselves means to love other and all. Each is interdependent on the others. Love is always unconditional and whole—Love As.

Every experience flows to and through us because of love—and through love, we are connected with everything. If self-love is disturbed through our stories of disconnect, we cannot experience the flow of love to other and to all. All disconnect begins within ourselves, therefore, all healing begins within ourselves. Through self-love we are a restored and inseparable, interconnected, and interdependent part of Love As.

I am Love As.

Other is Love As.

All is Love As.

5

A Story of Love, Power, and Purpose

When we have useful stories of purpose, power, and love, the pieces of a new story can connect; a story of unified love and power in service to purpose. This is the summarized story that revealed itself to me during a JournaLogue practice:

> The infinite realm of all being and becoming is spirit-consciousness-nature.
>
> Everything living that emerges within spirit-consciousness-nature has its inherent location, its sphere within this infinite realm. This sphere encompasses all that is there to be explored and expressed, the reason why it is there—the divine offering for its unique contribution.
>
> This unique contribution is its highest purpose.
>
> Everything is spirit-consciousness-nature, thus is interdependent and interconnected. This interdependence and interconnectedness is flowing energy—Love As.

Each exploration and expression of purpose depends on and is connected through and with Love As, and is therefore in service of self, other, and all.

Exploring and expressing ever more of our purpose is the process of self-realization, and this process flows with energy—with Power As, in service of self, other, and all.

Love and Power are the interconnected and interdependent energies of being and becoming in service of the infinite realm of spirit-consciousness-nature.

What had emerged for me was a story of love and power as neither separate, nor at odds with one another—but always present, and always together. This story holds the potential for us to embrace and embody our full authentic power, while at the same time being interconnected and interdependent through limitless love. Thus energized, we can embody our highest purpose in service of the infinite realm of all being and becoming.

Soon after this story formed in my awareness, I found myself triggered by an immense sense of overwhelm. What was I to do next? How could I integrate and express this story into my life? I was paralyzed by the feeling that this story could save the world. This brought sensations and thoughts of self-doubt, like, "who am I to save the world?" I thought of all the other writers and thinkers more qualified to tell a story like this.

I was in my next abyss, back to facing my demons. And, as life tends to present us with the learning opportunities we need, here's what happened next.

A life in balance

I had begun to work with a Social Enterprise in Africa. SINA Social Innovation Academy[24], based in Uganda, offers education to support marginalized youth in becoming social entrepreneurs. When I met a SINA founder in a workshop in Germany, I learned that SINA had begun working with Holacracy, implementing it by themselves. We agreed to collaborate, and three months later I was on a flight headed into Kampala.

I've done a fair bit of traveling in my life, but this was a very different place than what I could have imagined. It took me some days to adjust, and to overcome my own shyness. I knew that the people I was to meet, be they refugees or orphans, had lived on the streets, or had grown up in what I found to be unimaginable circumstances. I was painfully aware of my privilege.

Once I overcame my shyness and insecurity, I found a warm, friendly, and joyful crowd of wonderful people, who welcomed me in a way that felt like an embrace.

About a week after I arrived at SINA, I returned to my hut after a meeting. I had been told to lock my hut, as the compound could be entered by strangers from different sides.

The moment I entered my hut I felt something was strange. The back door was slightly ajar, and when I looked closer, I saw someone had smashed the glass and unfastened the bolt. I could feel shock and panic arise. After checking I found that I had been robbed of my money—an amount that was substantial for me, and that I had brought along in case I needed medical treatment or had an emergency.

It wasn't the loss of money that shook me deeply. In fact, the founders kindly offered reimbursement. What shook me was the sense of betrayal and loss of trust. I felt someone must have known that I would be away from my hut at a meeting—and that the thief might be known to me. There were about 50 or 60 people in the SINA compound. Who was I to trust, and who not?

---

[24] https://socialinnovationacademy.org/

During the next morning's community gathering, everyone was informed about what had happened. I was in tears, sharing how unsure I felt and how I was struggling with the issue of trust.

This meeting triggered two of my new friends into action. They had a suspicion and were going to see what they could learn. They begged me to not lose my trust and promised that they would find out who did this.

They did find the young man who had broken into my hut, and within three days he was in prison in the village near SINA. He was known to my friends, as he was a former member of SINA who had been asked to leave due to prior conduct. I was asked to go to the police station and make a statement, when a police officer asked if I would be willing to talk to the young man. I was confused. Why would I want to do that? The officer saw my confusion and immediately pulled back.

"It's ok," he said. "You really don't have to if you don't want to." I could feel that there was something I didn't understand, so I told the officer that if he needed me to come back, I would be happy to do that.

The next day, one of the two friends who had solved the case asked me again if I would be willing to talk to the imprisoned man. I still didn't understand why, but my friend said he would come with me and translate if necessary. Aware that I was missing something important, I agreed to go.

I was asked to sit on a chair in a corner of the room. Other people, meeting at a nearby table, were paying absolutely no attention to what was going on on my side of the room.

When the young man—let's call him Jeff—came in, I could see the fear on his face. His eyes darted about the room, unable to settle on me. He was made to sit on the floor right in front of me, which made me terribly uncomfortable. My friend spoke to Jeff, who eventually looked up at me and said, "I am sorry!".

I had no idea what to do with this, but it did start a conversation that included me. I learned that Jeff had lived in an orphanage until the age of 16. He had no real education but was a talented musician who loved to bring joy to children through making music with them. My friend took his mobile phone out and played me one of Jeff's songs.

Jeff's music touched something inside of me and my emotions started swirling through me like a raging river. I asked him what the hell he thought he was doing. How could he throw away his gifts like that? Wasn't he aware that going to jail would take him down a pathway he really didn't need in his life? Jeff was by then looking at me with his sad eyes, and he kept repeating, "I am sorry!".

Eventually my friend asked me, "do you accept his apology?". And that's when it hit me.

I had read about Restorative Justice, and though I didn't understand its applications in criminal law it dawned on me that this system was being used in Uganda. Understanding came over me. In short, I realized that if I accepted the apology of the offender, it would be seen as an act of reconciliation. The young man would be pardoned, and as a result would not have to face legal consequences.

Realization of what was at play welled up inside of me like a volcanic eruption. In this moment I was given complete power—over the life of this young man, hanging in the balance. Though he was the same age as my son, the two had led very, very different lives.

From a place deep inside of me came an answer—feeling more as though it emerged *through* me than *from* me. "Yes," I said. "Yes, I accept your apology, and I want something in exchange. I want us to make an agreement. I want you to promise that you will continue to make music, and with it bring joy to children. I want you to report back monthly to the police and tell them what you have been up to. I want you to promise that you will bring out an album of your music within a year. And I want you to promise that you won't steal anymore."

The police officer hand-wrote my request, and Jeff, the officer, and I all signed this paper. Then they led Jeff away. Before leaving the room, he turned around, now looking me in the eyes, and said, "thank you, Mom!" I knew he would be freed that day.

It took me some time, deep emotional processing, and many tears to integrate what had happened to me in my interactions with Jeff. I realized what a gift I had been given. Life had handed me a situation where I was given the power to decide another person's fate, possibly even as a matter of life or death as I learned later from my friend. From a place deep inside, without cognitive decision-making, I had acted from unified love and power. Though he still faces hurdles today, Jeff is making music, has published an album, and has created a foundation through which he works with children. In addition to bringing joy into their lives with music, Jeff tries to help children that he finds in desperate situations. In his way, Jeff too is now growing his capacity to act from unified love and power in service to his own purpose.

In reflecting on this experience, I reflected on the question of how I could access the source that had guided my answer in that police station—and how I could draw from it in an aware state, to let it guide me on my path of being and becoming.

This was so much more approachable than "saving the world"—this was experimenting and practicing a way of being, in everyday life, with things that could be quite mundane. How often do we react on autopilot, getting aggravated, annoyed, hurt, sad, or frustrated? How often do we blame or shame, playing out old patterns of behavior that we have developed in our lives? The practice of acting from unified love and power can become a way to explore whether a particular pattern is useful for us in our life, or if in this present moment we have other possible ways to act and react. Acting from unified love and power can create a new pattern, one that makes old patterns obsolete.

This whole exploration deeply influenced and added many new aspects to the JournaLogue practice. I visualized that place from which I felt guided back at the police station in Uganda, and it is now my "Sacred Space". This is where I return for my daily encounters with my "Inner Support Team". This team is composed of aspects of myself that are always there for me. They support me to learn ever more about anything that wants to be explored, and specifically about acting from unified love and power in service to my purpose.

Today I teach the JournaLogue practice as one manifestation of my purpose. This exploration can be as joyful as it is difficult. It invites us to look over and over again at our shadows and traumas. When grounded in the story of Love As, and the aspect that is self-love, we can remind ourselves that these shadows and traumas are just as important to who we are as all other aspects of our wholeness.

Emerging experiments

As my work led me into further exploration, many spaces emerged—one after the other—for experiments around the question, "how can the story of unified love and power express itself in service of the more-than-human world?"

I began to explore this question in collaboration with wonderful people all over the world. In constellation work, in conference settings, in in-person programs with participants from four different continents (the first "Love, Power and Purpose" program), and in various online settings, we looked from many angles and through many practices at this question. The most important aspect of these experiments was, and is, that the work begins with ourselves. No matter the size of the everyday task we are dealing with, be it significant or mundane, our response can be the same. If it causes us to disconnect (through anger, frustration, disappointment, fear, hurt, or other means), we can bring unified love and power into our present awareness and let a shift in our action emerge from this place—from where the unification is sourced.

Slowly, one after the other, new stories emerged from these spaces.

In one of my "Love, Power & Purpose" online sessions, James told us that for a very long time he had avoided visiting his parents. He couldn't face how his father kept telling him how he should be leading his life. He was so triggered by this behavior that each visit turned into a painful experience. He simply didn't want to experience this anymore.

After going through the sessions and practices, James told us he could now recognize a deep yearning to go and visit his parents and tell his father how much he loves him. Tears trickled down his face as he said this, but they were not tears of pain. His face clearly showed the joy and hope that this decision brought up for him. The tears came from beyond the pain that he had been holding for so long.

Later on, I learned that James did what he said he would. He visited his parents and told them both how much he loved them and how this was an incredibly healing experience.

Bettina, a woman from Germany, told me the following story during her JournaLogue Self-Coaching Training.

"I was last in line in a pharmacy, standing just inside the entrance and keeping my distance from the person in front of me (ah, Corona times!). A woman entered the pharmacy, walked past me, and stood a little off to the right ahead of me."

"I was in a hurry and my immediate reaction was to wonder why she wasn't respecting the line. I remember furrowing my brow and saying, "excuse me?!""

"She turned to me and said, also in an unfriendly tone, "I know you're in front of me in line. I'm just keeping my distance.""

"I immediately felt bad! I saw there wasn't room to stand behind me, and it was raining outside. Why would I immediately assume she was trying to jump the line? I realized that something had happened earlier that day to make me feel frustrated. That state of disconnect had carried over and caused me to be so unfriendly to the woman in the pharmacy."

"There, in the pharmacy, I closed my eyes and took a deep breath. I turned my awareness inward, connecting to my love and my power. The energy in my body changed and everything relaxed. I opened my eyes, turned to the woman, and told her how sorry I was for addressing her in this unfriendly way. Naturally, her body language and expression changed. She smiled at me. "Thank you," she said. "It's ok!"."

Bettina told me that in this unexpected, everyday moment, something inside of her shifted. She was able to develop a much deeper, felt sense of the potential that lies in acting from unified love and power—of experiencing herself as an interconnected and interdependent part of the "web of love"[25].

Things like this probably happen to all of us from time to time. No matter how much we have explored our shadow patterns, how aware we are of trauma and its impact on ourselves and others, life will continue to present us with learning opportunities.

In the first *Love, Power and Purpose* program, on Whidbey Island, Washington, USA, we went through a collective quest. We asked a guiding question to identify issues that we as a group wanted to address. "What can shift," we asked, "if we act from unified love and power in service of the more-than-human world?"

I will never forget the time we shared on that quest at the Whidbey Institute. Sharing stories and perspectives, drawing, painting, forming, playing, dancing, meditating, expressing ourselves through embodiment practices, journaling, walking, sharing meals, gathering around a campfire, singing together, crying, laughing—what an amazing container we collectively created.

As part of the process, everyone individually stepped over an artfully created threshold into the unknown, vocalizing their commitment to experimentation and their hope for how things could shift through acting from unified love and power. Among what emerged:

- Confidence to go into the dark and find the light.

- Commitment to wholeness, being and becoming and to the unknown.

---

[25] In a dialogue with my Love, I found that if it is love that "reveals the unity that is there", then it is love that reveals the web of life, which then also makes it the web of love. Hence the term was born and I use it frequently in my work.

- Dedication to equity, the environment, and the more-than-human world.

- Commitment to a life that contributes as the inseparable part of nature that we are.

- A promise to live with integrity, to find stillness and spaciousness, to allow the soul's passion and creativity to realize itself.

- A step into uncharted territory with unwavering trust.

- Undaunted courage for personal metamorphosis.

- Commitment to live every moment in awe of the miracle of it all.

- Capacity to hold soul centered wisdom, loving kindness, and compassion to all without bounds.

At the collective level, we asked, "what issues do we collectively feel called to experiment with? What might become possible? What new narratives might emerge for our families, our communities, our ecosystems, humanity, and the more-than-human world?"

What emerged was a visualization of possibility, the co-creation of new stories full of richness and beauty. We heard stories about:

- Drawing from ancient spiritual wisdom to refine the systems that support our livelihood, revisiting those learnings from today's perspective and bringing them together to nurture all of nature.

- Holding one another to standards that align with the well-being of the entire more-than-human world.

- Recognizing that what we experience in the present moment is what is necessary—that it enables us to sense what is needed next.

- Striving to live a purpose-guided life and holding agency for our soul potential.

- Embodying a life of "enoughness", where there is enough for everyone, while holding deep respect for the integrity of other living beings.

- Holding deep appreciation and gratitude for the life that is.

- Keeping equity at the core of all we do, valuing every individual regardless of background, identity, or circumstances.

- Seeing land not as owned, but tended to as a being with its own worth and sovereignty.

We explored each of those stories further, identifying where we—individually and collectively—could begin to experiment. We saw room for small experiments and new stories in parenting, education, arts, health, relationship to "ownership" (of nature, animals, and land), eating and growing food, local and global trading, community, technology, conflict, justice, economy, organizing, and governing. What emerged through our collective wisdom was tangible, inspiring, and possible.

This knowledge was omnipresent throughout this time together: our individual journey nourishes the collective journey, which nourishes our individual journey, which nourishes the collective journey. We are interconnected and interdependent. We need one another on this journey of being in powerful, loving relationships with self, other, and all.

The burden of not knowing

Our time together at Whidbey Institute was followed almost immediately by the COVID-19 pandemic—and the years that followed were very different than what many of us expected. My pattern of hosting workshops needed to shift away from in-person, international gatherings, and I turned to a quieter life of writing and coaching online. Meanwhile, the collective challenges facing humanity seemed to grow more rapid and complex with each passing month. I knew that this work around the unification of love and power in service to purpose was still relevant—perhaps more than ever—but I had questions. What did it all mean? What needed to happen next? What did the pathway forward, to integrate this new story, look like? I was, as Bayo Akomolafe[26] would put it, facing a crack.

At the heart of my questions was a sense that these things had to be addressed before I could continue writing. "After all," my thoughts said, "only the answers to these questions will make the book worth reading."

What a burden to hold! This story triggered all sorts of thought patterns that kept me trapped. "I have to." "I need to." "I should." Oh, I knew these old acquaintances, stepping out of my shadow again!

I did a great deal of journaling on these matters, and at one point my Inner Wisdom reminded me that I was on an archetypal Hero's Journey—and that at this point, I was traveling deep into an abyss. Others had been here before, and in recognizing it now, I could feel it. Stuck in the abyss, sitting in the crack, I could only accept and surrender. I knew this held the potential to let me see what was there for me to learn. When I stopped fighting my stuck feeling, I was able to reconnect with my curiosity. What would guide me through the abyss? What light might come through the crack, and what would it make visible?

I needed to explore the "not knowing" and this immediately gave rise to the next demon. It came in the form of new questions: how do I write about *not knowing*? How do I know about *not knowing*? This felt like an inescapable conundrum.

---

[26] https://www.bayoakomolafe.net/

The relief of not knowing

When I read about Bayo Akomolafe's program, "We Will Dance With the Mountains Into the Cracks", it felt like it was finding me exactly when I needed it. I had been following Akomolafe for some time and really admired his perspectives. My hope for the program was that it would help me go deep into the crack, to step completely out of every single one of my comfort zones, and to find what was there—under, over, and beyond.

In the first session we touched on experimenting and "failing forward"—concepts I've spent plenty of time with, and that I've integrated into my life through self-organization. While the material was familiar, I received an unexpected gift. Out of the stillness of a meditation, the light broke through the crack and my treasure revealed itself. The questions I had been holding turned into one obvious, very simple sentence. It emerged with so much power that I actually had to call it out: "I don't know!"

Not once, but repeatedly, I shouted, "I DON'T KNOW! I DON'T KNOW! I DON'T KNOW!"

Every time I called this sentence out, I felt increasing relief. I repeated it until I felt something inside of me shift.

There it was: the vastness, the liberation, the curiosity, the joy, the ease, the love, and the power of not knowing!

The light that now came through the crack shone on two things. First, a very old "friend" showed up—a Saboteur, resting deep down in my shadow. Second, a gift revealed itself—something that had been there all along, patiently waiting to be seen.

Thanks to my JournaLogue practice, meeting and befriending this Saboteur was quite easy. The pattern that had been holding me back had arisen from a sentence my sisters and I had heard over and over again from our parents: "think before you speak!" The subtext here was, "you're talking nonsense." Even heavier, "don't speak unless you know what you're talking about." There it is—I *need* to know.

This insight made it easy for me to let go of the issue entirely. Beyond lay something new, something intriguing, something exciting . . . and I was now ready to explore the unknown.

With the liberating energy of "I don't know", I could now see that I do have something very specific to share. It has nothing to do with knowing, but with inviting others into experimentation with the unknown. I have been, and am, creating individual and collective spaces to allow for and hold the unknown. With others around the globe, I'm making room for what wants to emerge. For failing forward. For letting go and letting come. For all of this at the same time.

I invite you to join an individual and collective journey around the question, "what becomes possible when we act from unified love and power in service of the greater whole?" Join us in building a global community that travels this interdependent and interconnected journey with self, other, and all!

The invitation

Hello, dear reader. Christiane here. You've heard so many different stories from my life and others' lives. From here forward I invite you into an experience that's all about you—your inner life, your own love, power, and purpose, and your relationship with self, other, and all.

It is an invitation to contribute through your individual stories, to co-create new stories, and to embody the unification of love and power in service of the more-than-human world. The following chapters detail ways to join this movement.

First, you will learn about the JournaLogue practice for self-coaching. The next chapter includes a detailed description of all foundational steps of the JournaLogue practice, as well as some stories about how the practice emerged and it supports the process of diving into the unknown, experimenting, failing forward, and learning to act from unified love and power.

Second, you'll see possibilities for how to join and contribute to the growth of a global community. Be part of a co-creative collective sharing new stories, in the words of Charles Eisenstein, about this "beautiful world our heart knows is possible."[27]

---

[27] Recommended read: Charles Eisenstein: "The More Beautiful World Our Heart Knows Is Possible"; North Atlantic Books (5 Nov. 2013)

6

The JournaLogue

> "Try not to resist the changes that come your way.
> Instead let life live through you.
> And do not worry that your life is turning upside down.
> How do you know that the side you are used to is better than
> the one to come?"
> —Rumi

The JournaLogue is a self-coaching practice. It offers you a way to experiment with embodying your purpose in a powerful and loving way. It is the basis from which I'll invite you into collective experimentation with the unification of love and power to shift larger issues that matter to you, to others, and to the more-than-human world . . . but let me come back to that later!

I am so grateful for the many people who have inspired me during the development of this practice, which emerged through the experiences and learnings I've described herein. I've named many of my teachers in this book—and to those wise ones not named, I also offer my humble gratitude.

The word JournaLogue is a combination of "journaling" and "dialogue". This is a journaling practice through which one builds connection, trust, and meaningful relationship with a group of one's inner parts and transcribes one's dialogue with them.

The concept of "parts" used here draws from Carl Jung's work on Archetypes and is inspired by the teachings of Carolyn Myss, Carol Pearson, Stacey Couch, and Robert Ohotto. The dialogue part of the practice draws from a number of different teachings, such as Voice Dialogue[28], David Bohm's Dialog[29], generative listening[30], and others.

"Dialogue" is often misinterpreted as a conversation between two people. The roots of the word come from the Greek words of "dia" and "logos". "Dia" means "through" and "logos" translates to "word" or "meaning". In essence, a dialogue is a flow of meaning. In the most ancient meaning of the word, "logos" meant "to gather together" and suggested an intimate awareness of relationship. Deriving from that, the dialogue of the JournaLogue practice is intended to be a flow of meaning in relationships.

Journaling can be done in many different forms: writing, drawing, painting, moving, dancing, speaking, singing, shaping, or assembling artifacts. Journaling can take any form of artful expression. Nonetheless, my invitation is to begin by journaling through writing. If you would like to use other artful expressions, you may. In the beginning, please combine these expressions with writing. A primary reason is that there are points in the JournaLogue practice when you'll be invited to go back and read what you've written.

Eventually, you might develop your very own form and expression of the JournaLogue. You may let that emerge from the early practice, as described here.

The JournaLogue foundation program offered here is a step-by-step process. While the natural phenomena of learning,

---

[28] https://www.voicedialogueinternational.com/
[29] David Bohm: On Dialogue; Routledge; 1st edition (September 19, 2013)
[30] https://psgedmundrice.files.wordpress.com/2019/01/generative-listening.pdf

development, and growth are not linear, there is value in this context of doing one step first, then building on this step with the next. Think of learning to play an instrument, or any sport. A series of specific practices that build upon one another brings flow.

To get the most out of this foundation program, please follow the exercises as you read them—one after the other. You can do this entirely at your own pace. One way is to make it a daily practice.

The JournaLogue exercises will take you an average of 30 to 45 minutes. Some choose to read the lesson in the evening, then do the exercise the next morning. If you don't have time to make this a daily practice, you might give yourself a few days for each exercise. Sometimes it can be useful to stay with one exercise and repeat it until you feel ready to move on. It really is entirely up to you.

If you decide to read through the rest of this book before coming back to the JournaLogue, that's fine too. Once you do begin, however, you'll be best served if you do the exercises in the sequence they are described. You might miss out on some important insights if you leave out exercises. My invitation: trust the process.

The JournaLogue practice is about tapping into the unknown, about embracing the unknown, about trusting emergence, about letting light come through the cracks. When the moment is right, it's about experimenting and about failing forward.

While leaving room for this emergence, hold love for your cognition. Your cognitive thoughts generally emerge from what you already know. Allow them to be a part of the journey, but not the only resource. Let them travel hand-in-hand with the very different kind of wisdom that you will be accessing.

There's one more important piece of guidance for your journaling: as soon as you begin writing, don't stop. Don't think about what you want to write next, don't try to formulate a nice, correct, or meaningful sentence that best expresses what is on your mind, and don't delete what you have already written. Just keep writing.

In the beginning, this might not be easy. Shortly, however, you will begin to see how this practice helps you to open up to the voices that come from beyond your habitual thinking.

Here's a part of my early journal, in dialogue with Inner Wisdom, which I'll share as an example:

Me: I don't know what's up with me today. I feel restless and can't focus. Why is that? Why is that? Why is that? I hate it when that happens. I really don't know what to write. I started with a question, but now I can't remember that question. I hate it when that happens. I am frustrated. I hate it when that happens.

IW, please can you help me? I am so frustrated. I remember that I had a question because of a dream I had. The question was there this morning when I woke up and I remember it felt really important. But I can't remember. That is driving me crazy. IW, please help me!

IW: Keep writing.

Me: What? Really? Oh boy, I think I expected that from you. Ok, I'll just keep writing. But I don't know what to write. All I can think of is asking you for help.

IW: I am helping you. Please just keep writing.

Me: I don't know what to do. I don't know what to write. I don't know what to write. I am so frustrated. Where does the frustration come from?

IW: Now you're getting somewhere.

Me: The frustration. The frustration. Why am I so frustrated? OMG—I just realized my frustration has nothing to do with the fact that I can't remember the question of this morning. I am still holding some anger about what happened yesterday.

IW: There you go. Now you've arrived where you need to be right now.

For the remainder of that journaling session, I was able to continue with a very fruitful dialogue that helped me resolve an issue I had been stuck with for some time.

I learned two things from Julia Cameron's "The Artist's Way" which I've integrated into the JournaLogue practice. One is what I just described: don't stop writing. The other relates to the recommended length for a journaling session. Julia Cameron suggests three pages of longhand writing. When I was still journaling with handwriting, I took that to be three letter size pages. Once I shifted to journaling on my laptop, I found a website called 750 Words, and in my early practice days this was very useful. While I no longer use the website, I still find that about 750 words is a good goal for those typing their journals. It takes some practice to fill three pages of your journal or type 750 words before you stop writing.

In the beginning of the JournaLogue, you will be asked to journal for a specific duration, no matter how much you write. Then, instructions will guide you toward three pages or 750 words. Eventually, you will find your own useful path.

Journaling as a spiritual practice

Journaling as a daily practice is recommended and practiced by many, across cultures. I practice the JournaLogue daily, and it has become a very important part of my life. Before settling on a pattern that serves me well, I went through periods of consistent, daily writing or occasional writing. I dropped out for long periods of times, then resumed writing, daily or intermittently. Eventually it became what it is for me now: a daily gift, and a vital self-care practice. On the few occasions when I don't journal—when I travel or have a very early commitment—I feel I am missing out on something. I am always very happy to resume my daily practice as soon as possible.

There was a pattern—invisible to me, at first—around when I dropped out of my journaling practice for longer periods. In retrospect, I can see that it happened when I was facing some uncomfortable, or even painful, issues. I wasn't ready to face these issues then. Today I have learned to deal with similar situations in a different way. Rather than stop journaling, I talk to the part that is most concerned with the issue at hand. I tell that part that I am not ready to face this, and to give me time to come back to it when I feel ready.

This always works. I know the issue is there, waiting to be dealt with, but I experience no pressure. Eventually I always come back to it—sometimes in small steps, and sometimes at full speed. Either way, I know I need not face it until I'm ready.

Coming back to the frequency of practicing the JournaLogue, many find the daily practice to be a deep and very helpful experience. I recommend it wholeheartedly. We all have to find our own way, though, so please experiment with what works for you. Invite yourself to step outside of your comfort zone. If possible, try to journal every morning, or at another suitable time of the day, and see where it takes you.

I recently heard from Jackie, an American woman who participated in a *30-Day JournaLogue Intensive* course some years ago. At the time, she had shared that the material was interesting and helpful but that she was struggling to make it a daily practice in her busy life.

Nonetheless, the lessons of the JournaLogue practice stayed with Jackie and her Inner Support Team is still with her after pauses in the practice. She reached out to me this month after having what she called an "astonishing" JournaLogue session.

Jackie turned back to her Inner Wisdom in a time of crisis.

"A few weeks ago, I was devastated by something really challenging in my personal life and I felt so afraid and alone. All my old fears and anxieties were being triggered. I couldn't sleep or focus on work, so I took out my journal and began to write to my Inner Wisdom—I really didn't know what else to do."

Jackie shared with me that despite the long pause she had made, her Inner Wisdom was right there, ready to speak with her. The words flowed and before long she had three pages of rich handwritten dialogue filled with gems of insightful loving guidance, plus powerful and simple methods to care for herself and her loved ones through the heartbreak. Best of all, the wisdom she tapped into has stayed with her and helped resource her to have a wonderful month despite external circumstances beyond her control.

If you've read this far, you're ready for the step-by step JournaLogue foundation program. To build the practice, you will be taken through three phases, of which each has a set of exercises. For each exercise you will first read an overview framing what it is about, followed by a detailed description of how to go through the exercise.

Two ways to proceed

If you want to learn the core JournaLogue practice by experiencing exercises as you read through this book, I suggest you first read the overview and the detailed description of each exercise. Then, before reading further, go back to the beginning of the detailed description, entitled "The Exercise", and follow the prompts as described.

If you want to finish reading the whole book first and then come back to doing the JournaLogue practices, that will work as well. If taking this approach, please be aware that some exercises refer to the outcomes of earlier steps. This might create a lack of clarity while reading. Just know that you'll get more clarity when you come back to do the JournaLogue.

Once you decide to begin the JournaLogue practice, know that you are never alone. If you sign into lppexperiments.global you can participate in practice groups for each of the three phases of the JournaLogue. You can ask questions about the practice, read what other practitioners share, share your own experiences, participate in practice group calls, and more! You will also find more resources for the practice, including additional exercises.

Phase 1: Outer and Inner Conditions

Exercise I: getting started

> "The single most sacred pilgrimage
> you will ever make
> is the one right where you are."
> —Molly Kate Brown

The JournaLogue practice begins with creating supportive conditions.

Much of your practice time is spent journaling. In order to stay focused and present with this practice, you'll adopt a few rituals. Some support you in creating the outer conditions for the practice, and others support you in creating your inner conditions.

We begin with creating the outer conditions.

Where?

Please find a place where you love to sit, where you are very comfortable, and where you will always be undisturbed during your practice. Dedicate this place to your practice and set an intention to always return to it to do your JournaLogue. If you travel, bring the same level of awareness and intention to choosing a temporary JournaLogue spot so that each place best serves you, wherever you are.

Make sure you are not distracted by your tech devices. If you are journaling on your laptop, turn on the "do not disturb" function so you don't receive notifications. If you use your mobile phone for music or timing, turn off notifications and place it face down.

In your dedicated place, you might want to add some ambiance. Consider candles, flowers, some meaningful memorabilia, or incense. Maybe you have a singing bowl or a tuneful bell with which you want to begin and end your sessions. Bring whatever items you like if they will hold the space with you. These meaningful objects can help you stay present and focused when you practice. If you travel a lot, try and find at least one item that you can take with you—this can support you in getting present with your practice, wherever you go.

Choose specific, instrumental music to play in the background or on earphones. Please choose something that won't distract you, and that won't make you want to hum along. Lyrics are too distracting. Try music designed for meditation or concentration. You can find many suitable playlists on many online music platforms. I use an app called "Insight Timer". The free version provides guided meditation as well as music that supports relaxation, meditation, and sleep. It is helpful to always play the same music while doing the JournaLogue exercises.

For some people, any kind of music, even relaxation and meditation music, is a distraction. If you prefer complete silence, then go with what supports you best.

How?

Different people have different preferences on how to journal. Some write in a journal or notebook, using a favorite pen or pencil. Some like to journal on a laptop, tablet, or desktop. You might not want to write at all, but prefer to speak your journal entries into a recorder. For our practice, it really doesn't make a difference. Just make a conscious decision about how to proceed and try to be consistent from one session to the next. While it's fine to combine the journaling with any other art form, learning the foundations of the JournaLogue will be most successful if you write (or record) during each session.

Whether working online or on paper, make sure to keep your JournaLogue resources and entries together in one place—either a physical journal or folder, or a digital folder. These will stay with you for the duration of the JournaLogue foundation program, and beyond.

When?

When to do your daily assignments is up to you. I suggest the morning, since it is often easiest to reserve time before we step into our normal, everyday rhythm. You might have a different morning practice that you don't want to change, or you simply might not be up to it in the morning. If that's the case, choose another time that works consistently for you. In any case, the important thing is to make your practice as regular as possible.

An important note

Your journal is for your eyes only! It is important that you let the words flow—honest and unfiltered. If we fear that others will read what we write, or feel we need to write for others, what comes will not be pure and authentic. It doesn't matter if what you write is grammatically incorrect, if you make spelling or typing mistakes, or if the sentences don't make any sense. That is all completely irrelevant. You are only writing for yourself.

How to begin?

You have created your outer conditions—now, it's time to look inward. What inner conditions can support you in getting started?

If you have a mindfulness or meditation practice, it can be wonderful to move straight from your practice to the JournaLogue exercise.

If you don't follow a specific mindfulness practice, then I suggest you do a short breathing exercise to center yourself before you get started. For example: take four very deep breaths, all the way down into your belly. Slowly, in through your nose . . . hold briefly . . . slowly out through your mouth . . . hold briefly . . . slowly in through your nose . . . hold briefly . . . and so on. After four deep breaths in and out, pay attention to how your breath returns to its normal rhythm and flow. Stay with this attunement to breath for about 30 seconds. Then you're ready to get started.

The exercise

Your first exercise is preparing the outer conditions and inner conditions.

Find and define your dedicated place—the spot you will always return to when you do the JournaLogue practices (unless you are traveling).

Prepare your journal. A book, notebook, or paper pad, and a favorite pen to write with. Alternatively, you can create a folder on your tablet or laptop or decide to journal with a specific app (Evernote, Ulysses, or the like).

If you feel that it can contribute to the atmosphere of your dedicated space, place candles, memorabilia, pieces of art, or any other artifacts that are meaningful to you.

Unless you prefer total silence, choose suitable instrumental music to play in the background. You will always play the same music, so it's good to create a playlist.

Sense into the space. Is there anything else you feel would help create just the right conditions for you to go through the exercises of the JournaLogue?

Once you have done all that, take a few minutes to sit in your JournaLogue place. Welcome the place and yourself in it. Set your intention to come here, in your own rhythm, at a certain time, for the duration of your JournaLogue foundation program (and maybe beyond). Set your intention to build your individual practice to experiment with acting from unified love and power in service to your purpose and the more-than human-world.

Take a few moments to sense into your personal purpose. You might have a high level of awareness about how your purpose is currently expressing itself, or you may have only a murky idea of what you are here to do. Any sense that you currently have of it is fine for our practice.

Next you are invited to journal the answers to two questions:

1) How does my personal purpose currently express itself?

Please be aware that this is not about a perfect statement. You will not be required to talk to others about it, unless you want to. Remember, your journal is entirely private to you. If you are not clear about your purpose yet, it is perfectly fine to write something like, "I think my purpose is about . . .," or, "my purpose is something having to do with . . .."

2) How do I feel now about beginning the JournaLogue?

Set your timer for 15 minutes and start writing immediately. Try and sense into the answer, not thinking about it too much. Practice writing without stopping. What you write doesn't have to make sense in a cognitive way. Here are suggestions about how you can journal today:

- Describe how you feel now. Are you hesitant, excited, or anxious?
- What are your hopes and fears about the JournaLogue (if any)?
- What is your intention—why are you beginning the JournaLogue?
- What questions are you currently holding about the practice?

These are just suggestions. Just hold the questions and see what emerges.

When the timer tells you that you're done, you have created the outer conditions and have begun to set up your inner conditions. You are now set up for the JournaLogue.

Welcome to the journey!

Exercise II: your Sacred Space

> "Your Sacred Space
> is where you can find yourself
> again, and again."
> —Joseph Campbell

Early on, I often found myself not really being able to get started with the JournaLogue practice. Even though I meditated and did breathing practices before starting, two things kept coming up: either my head would spin with many thoughts about what I would or should be writing or would worry about how I could make sure that the journaling session would be rich and meaningful, bringing me deep insights as it had done so many times before. That was a huge roadblock for me over and over again.

When I went on journaling while holding all these expectations, the practice never lived up to its potential. Later, reading what I had written in such a state, I was always disappointed. My journal entries from those days were heady and uninteresting. All I had done was try to write things that, a) I already knew, and b) I thought made me sound interesting and intelligent. That was not what I wanted.

I began to experiment with overcoming this through trial and error. I began to develop a sense that, as we go into deep introspection and self-reflection, we connect to a sphere somewhere deep inside of us. It is the sphere where we can connect with our infinite wisdom, the gateway to our soul.

What I did then was to visualize this sphere. With the help of an Inner Support Team (which you will soon learn more about) I developed a self-guided meditation that led me into this absolutely stunning inner space, filled with endless natural beauty and with a very unique ambiance of light, sounds, smells, tastes, and other sensations of comfort.

As this image and the feelings it evoked built up, I knew I was arriving in my own true, inner Sacred Space. That's how I know it, but you'll find your own sensations and your own words. If the term "Sacred Space" isn't suitable for you, please find your own name for what you discover, and with which you can continue in your JournaLogue. I will invite you to go through the visualization to give rise and access to your own unique Sacred Space.

The Exercise

What follows is the transcript of a guided meditation to visualize your Sacred Space. There are a number of ways you can choose to use this. Maybe it is enough for you to slowly read the transcript and, in parallel, be aware of how your Sacred Space emerges—in images and sensations, in your body, mind, heart, and spirit.

If you are used to listening to guided meditations, you may choose to listen to this one. You can invite someone who knows about guided meditation and visualization to read the meditation to you. You can record yourself reading the transcript, and then listen to your own recording, or you can go to lovepowerandpurpose.com/resources and find the Sacred Space Guided Meditation that is freely available.

The Sacred Space Meditation

Find a comfortable position, sitting or lying down. When you're ready, gently close your eyes.

Take a few deep breaths – in through the nose . . . hold . . . out through the mouth . . . hold . . . in through the nose . . . hold . . . out through the mouth. Feel how, when you breathe in, relaxation flows into your body. When you breathe out, any tension you might hold in your body flows out.

Now allow your breath to take its own rhythm. Effortlessly flowing, in . . . and . . . out . . . in . . .

In your imagination, you are strolling on a path. One after the other, you can see elements of a landscape arise. This can be a large meadow . . . or mountains . . . maybe you're on a beach, or maybe a desert, or an oasis... it is your landscape that you enjoy strolling through.

As you are walking through this lovely landscape . . . slowly, mindfully . . . with every step, you become aware of more and more details.

Peacefully walking along, you approach a wall made of natural rocks of all sizes, with flowers and little bushes growing out of the cracks between the rocks. As you get closer, you can see a wooden gate. As you see the gate, it quietly opens and invites you to step in.

You step through it, and what opens up in front of you is an amazingly beautiful, lush garden. As you walk into the garden you can see that everything here is almost magical ... the beautiful trees, so alive, waving their branches at you in greeting. The high grass and the flowers, softly swaying in the gentle breeze. A little river with a friendly babble, birds singing their songs and tweeting, bees buzzing, and maybe rabbits, deer, or other animals. Maybe even mythical animals . . . one after the other, they peacefully turn their head towards you to greet you and then they go about their ways.

You walk closer to the babbling brook . . . and now you can see a small, beautiful building. Is it a wooden pagoda . . . or a temple . . . or maybe a simple wooden hut? A cave, a church, or a tent? What is it for you? Take a moment to become fully aware of the beauty of your building, and sense how it invites you in. You follow that invitation and step inside. Inside there are many comfortable opportunities to settle down—cushions in different sizes and colors, armchairs, loungers, all laid out in a circle. There is this one place that you feel drawn to, and you sit down. As you sit down and settle in, you can feel how your whole body relaxes even more.

You are enjoying this sense of total relaxation and are now becoming aware of even more details of your space . . . the light . . . the colors . . . maybe even sounds . . . all the details of this beautiful place you have arrived at. This is the place you will return to every time you do your JournaLogue practice . . . it is your own, unique Sacred Space.

When you feel you have full awareness of your Sacred Space and feel complete, you are ready to begin your return journey.

Stepping out of your Sacred Space . . . walking back through the magical garden . . . out through the gate . . . back through your landscape . . .

Take a deep breath . . . and in your own time, start moving your fingers, wiggling your toes, and beginning to move your whole body. When you are ready, fully bring your awareness back into the present moment through opening your eyes.

Once you have fully returned from this excursion, there's one more small thing to do. Find your own artful expression through which you can anchor the experience of your Sacred Space. You can write about it in your journal; draw or paint it; speak, hum, or sing; dance, shape, or form; collage or assemble; or maybe just quietly sit with it. Recall the experience of being in your Sacred Space and find an expression of it in any form you like. This is a space you will return to again and again for your JournaLogue practice. From now on, all JournaLogue conversations about how to experiment with acting from unified love and power in service to purpose will happen in this space.

It is important that you practice returning to your Sacred Space. You can do this any time during the day, not only during your JournaLogue sessions. Simply close your eyes and reconnect to the sensations and images of your Sacred Space, as you experienced it in your visualization.

When you feel that you can always return to your Sacred Space at the beginning of your JournaLogue practice, you are ready to move on to the next exercise.

Exercise III: your personal SCENARIO

> "Stress comes from the fear of the unknown;
> tranquility comes from accepting the unknown
> with love and joy."
> —Debasish Mridha

The JournaLogue is a practice that invites us into the unknown, and to hold the question, "how does my experience shift when I act from unified love and power?"

In order to explore this question, we begin with one specific experiment. We will do a number of smaller experiments as well, so to avoid confusion we call the larger, personal experiment your SCENARIO.

Prototyping is a way to experiment with the unknown. Today's exercise is about identifying what your SCENARIO will be and using it as a prototype for shifting into a place of unified love and power in relation to any issue or challenge that arises in our life. This exercise supports you to decide on one specific situation or relationship which, in the past, has been unpleasant, or may even be causing you emotional pain. This situation or relationship should be one in which you would like to shift into a better experience through acting from unified love and power in the future.

To prepare for this exercise, please choose a specific situation that you have encountered repeatedly in your life, where the experience has made you feel bad (perhaps angry, frustrated, sad, hurt, disappointed, let down, unheard, or disrespected). Alternatively, is there a specific person with whom you've had repeated unpleasant interactions? Choose a situation or a person (maybe they are connected) with which, or with whom, you would have liked to have acted and felt differently—maybe more loving and powerful, calmer and more resourceful—in the past. For whatever reason, the situation keeps repeating itself in an unpleasant way.

Please be kind to yourself. Choose a situation and/or person you know you will be facing, ideally while you are going through the JournaLogue foundation program. A situation that you are willing to experiment with and to prepare yourself for. Choose something which connects you to your desire to change, through acting in a more loving and powerful (thus authentic) way. At the same time, make sure this person or situation doesn't feel totally overwhelming.

Once you feel you have found a suitable situation and/or person, ask yourself:

- Would I like to have the resources to shift this situation/encounters with this person into a pleasant or even joyful experience?
- Would I like to find a pathway to experiment with this shift?

If the answer to either of these questions is no, then please try to find another situation and/or person.

Once the answer to both questions is yes, congratulations! You have identified your SCENARIO, with which you will experiment and explore how to shift any situation into a loving and powerful experience.

If you'd like to be guided through the following visualization, you can go to lovepowerandpurpose.com/resources and listen to the guided visualization that is offered there for this step of the process.

The Exercise

Settle into your dedicated space and do everything you need to get started. Get your journal ready, prepare candles and/or music, do some meditation or breathing, and prepare in any other way that you need to step into this undisturbed time for yourself.

Now lean back, close your eyes, and go on an imaginative journey. Imagine what you are doing in your Scenario, your prototypical situation/relationship. Imagine the situation or encounter in the future, where everything is shifting. Imagine it unfolding as a pleasant experience. Visualize it as you would like it to be. Let it play out in that way.

Visualize the context: Where will you be? What might the room or the place look like? What will the occasion be? What will you hear, smell, or taste? How will you feel? Who will you talk to? What will be the subject of your conversation? How are you and others acting, talking, and behaving? Let the feeling of being loving and powerful at the same time emerge, to the greatest extent possible.

If it is difficult for you to visualize the situation with closed eyes, you can also do it in a different way. Identify something that can function as an imaginary television screen (represented by a picture on the wall, the door of a closet, or anything rectangular that could represent a screen—NOT the screen of your computer, if you are typing your journal.

Now watch that space, and imagine that your situation plays as desired, like a video, on this "screen". Watch it in every detail. Enjoy watching yourself from this observer perspective, while your behavior is loving and powerful.

Be patient and kind with yourself! This is only the beginning. If it is difficult for you to imagine this situation to happen in a good way, or the relationship to feel good, simply repeat to yourself, "I will experiment with this situation. I will try to shift it through acting from unified love and power."

At this point of the JournaLogue practice, your main goals are identifying your SCENARIO and setting the intention to shift your experience. If you can't imagine yet how this situation or the interaction with this specific person can shift into a pleasant experience, please don't worry—that's completely ok. Just identify the situation or person, and set your intention.

Once you feel you are really imagining your SCENARIO and have a clear sense of your intention—or maybe you can even visualize the new situation—open your journal and start writing. Describe your SCENARIO and tell the story.

Here's how to do it:

- Set your timer for 30 or 40 minutes.
- Write the headline: "My SCENARIO".
- Start journaling immediately–just write freely.
- Connect back to your visualization. Let the words flow, unfiltered and unedited.
- Write everything that comes up and keep writing for the entire time. Don't stop. Keep writing. How does the thought of the situation or relationship make you feel? How would it feel to shift this situation or relationship? Are there fears or concerns you have about experimenting with this situation and/or person?
- Write down as many details as you can. Describe the future situation as it shows up for you in your visualization. If you can't visualize it, simply describe it in the way you feel you would like it to be.
- If something else comes up, write that down as well.

There is no right or wrong! All you need for this exercise is an idea of your SCENARIO, so that you know where you are heading with the JournaLogue foundation program. It doesn't matter how complete your description is—what you have at this point is all you need. The rest of the story, though it might not be written down, is in your mind, heart, and soul. Trust me. Better yet, trust yourself!

When you reach the end of your time, there's only one more thing to do: Give your SCENARIO a name.

Any name is fine! The name is a placeholder, something to identify the SCENARIO that you are going to prepare yourself for in the course of this JournaLogue. The name will help you to refer to it in a short manner and will hold the whole story that you visualized. You could of course just call it "My SCENARIO".

Sense into it a bit. Maybe a more specific name can make it even more personal to you, or maybe not. Either way is fine.

You may have noticed that the word SCENARIO is sometimes written in capital letters and sometimes in lower case. You will find this difference in connection with different words throughout the practice. Here's why.

Every time you see a word written in caps, this means that it addresses something that is personal to you. In the case of scenario—when written in lower case, the word means scenarios in general, but when it's written SCENARIO it addresses your unique personal SCENARIO, which you will experiment with in this JournaLogue program. If you have given your SCENARIO a name, then SCENARIO is a placeholder for the name you have given it.

In the case of love, when written in lower case it points to all love—Love AS, as you read in the chapter "The Story of Love". When it is written LOVE, it addresses the part of YOU that is LOVE. The part of you through which you are connected to Love AS. The same goes with power and POWER, and other parts as well.

This was a lot of information, so let me recap the steps of this exercise:

- Identify the situation and/or person that is going to be your SCENARIO

- Visualize, as well as you can, how your SCENARIO means shifting a specific situation or relationship into a pleasant experience.

- Do a journaling session to describe your SCENARIO.

- Give your SCENARIO a name.

When all this is done, you have reached the end of Phase 1 and are ready to move on to the next phase of the JournaLogue foundation program.

Phase 2: Your Inner Support Team

Exercise IV: connecting to SOURCE

> "Like an ability or a muscle,
> hearing your inner wisdom
> is strengthened by doing it."
> —Robbie Gass

The JournaLogue, like many other contemplative practices, can be seen as a journey. It is a journey we embark on without knowing where it will take us. This can be both exhilarating and scary. We are invited to hold the unknown, to remain grounded in our curiosity and our "beginner's mind", and to allow space for emergence.

The JournaLogue is both an inner individual and outer collective journey. Of course, those are never separate, but for our practice it is useful to differentiate these perspectives. We can look at and reflect on the inner aspects of our journey and do the same with the outer, collective aspects of it—the aspects that relate to the other people in our lives, be they colleagues, family members, friends, or people who share our passion—perhaps people we've not even yet met. In neither case are we alone. We have both inner and outer travel companions.

In the beginning we focus on our inner aspects. At some point, either through your own curiosity or through the exercises that follow, you will be invited to take a deeper look at the outer aspects—the way you engage with those around you and share collective experiences. This is how your experiments will happen. You'll bring these experiences back to inform the inner part of the journey, through reflection and introspection. On the way to experiencing the unification of love and power in your SCENARIO, which you identified in the last exercise, we will do a few smaller exercises to move in that general direction. Each of those experiments will take you on the "dance" of inner and outer experience.

On your inner journey you will meet a variety of travel companions. I promise that you are up for some really interesting and inspiring encounters. On this journey, you'll have conversations of a sort you may never have had before.

At this point on the JournaLogue journey, you'll be connecting to your primary travel companion. You may or may not know that this companion has been with you, and will be with you, for your entire life.

Allow me to introduce your SOURCE!

Your SOURCE is the part inside of you through which you have access to the entirety of wisdom . . . the wisdom that you *have always* had access to, the wisdom that you *will always* have access to, and all the wisdom that is there for you to discover. Through your SOURCE you are connected to the infinite realm of all being and becoming. Your SOURCE gives you access to explore and encounter your soul.

Our SOURCE is ever present and ready to connect when we search for answers within ourselves. The means to talk to the SOURCE (as to all our other parts) are self-reflection and introspection. The SOURCE is always there and ready to be addressed directly.

The SOURCE helps us to recognize our preconceived ideas, judgements, and evaluations and to go beyond all those preconceptions. Through this we gain access to the deeper wisdom that is ours to learn from and explore.

When I first started my journaling practice, all I did was to sit down and capture what was going on in my head. It was almost like talking to myself and often ended up being more like a diary. This very soon began to bore me. Honestly, who likes being bored? I eventually gave up the practice.

At the time, I didn't know that I could actually invite my SOURCE (and, as it soon turned out, every one of my parts) into a conversation—a dialogue about anything I was curious about or needed help with.

When I was introduced to different forms of "Voice Dialogue" it dawned on me that this could be a way to make journaling a much richer experience. Discovering this practice changed my life.

When I began experimenting with JournaLogue writing, I found some of the dialogues with my parts—and especially with the SOURCE—to be difficult. I didn't know how to start the conversations. As strange as it might sound, I was sometimes shy and insecure. The practice felt weird. I soon discovered that getting to know my inner parts is no different from getting to know anybody in the outside world. With some it's easy, with others less so.

While I know there is no "one size fits all" approach, I have found certain patterns that have helped me and many of my clients to build wonderful relationships with the SOURCE and an inspiring cast of other parts.

When I teach the JournaLogue I use the descriptive term SOURCE, because to me it appears to be the least biased way of describing this part. My SOURCE is actually called "Inner Wisdom". When journaling, I use the abbreviation IW. My IW is neither masculine, nor feminine. Defining its identity more clearly is completely unimportant.

Your SOURCE might be called something different. It might be one of many things—an animal or a plant, an Angel, a mythical creature, God, a beam of light, a sound, or a deceased relative. There are innumerable possibilities for how your SOURCE enters your awareness. You will discover more as you dialogue with your SOURCE in your journal.

Even after years of being in dialogue with my SOURCE (called IW), what is revealed through the experience never ceases to amaze me.

For every one of us, these dialogues develop in a very personal and unique way. Nonetheless, I am often asked by clients to share examples from my journal. Here's one such example—a dialogue with my IW that turned out to be particularly helpful to me.

On this particular morning, I had realized that sometimes something was in the way of me getting into the journaling flow.

It felt like I was stuck in some kind of confusion. I turned to my IW, and here's what happened:

Me: IW, can you please help me? How can I become aware of what is available for me now?

IW: That's the wrong question here.

Me: Can you help me with the question? What would be the right question?

IW: Are you assuming that I will give you the answer to this question?

Me: Yes, I was, and I am getting a sense that it's not what I am going to get from you now, right?

IW: Right.

Me: Ok, I will take a deep breath and try and sense into the answer for myself. . . . Now I realize that it is hard for me to let go of the expectation that there "should" be something there.

IW: So, what is it that seems to be in your way?

Me: What was it I said before? Oh yes, the expectations. I guess I have been "spoiled" by the number of lovely things that I have been able to explore while journaling lately and I have developed a form of hunger for it. Now I expect something special to happen every time.

IW: I get it, but do you realize that your expectations override the freshness of your curiosity?

Me: I understand that very well. Still, it's a challenge for me to let go of the expectations and accept the emptiness. While trying, there is that thought in the back of my mind that says, "Keep journaling and you will have access to more meaningful things". Ah, what I am hearing now very clearly is, "stay calm, breathe . . . hold the emptiness!" I hear you, IW.

IW: I'm glad you are getting it. It's about holding the emptiness for the sake of the emptiness, not for the expectation of something to come and fill the emptiness. When expectations fill the emptiness, they become the obstacle for what really wants to emerge.

This dialogue helped me to see how often my expectations get in the way of being present in the moment and giving space for emergence.

It is quite possible, of course, that you are already in communication with your SOURCE. In this case, please use this first exercise to reconnect and to have a dialogue about the upcoming journey with the JournaLogue.

I will continue to use SOURCE as a descriptive, so please while you are reading, always make sure to mentally substitute this with the name or description that is *your* part, *your* infinite wisdom, *your* connection to your soul.

The Exercise

- As always, please begin with either a short meditation or a breathing exercise.
- Set your timer to 30 minutes (or longer if you feel like it).
- Open your journal and put the headline, "Meeting my SOURCE".
- Close your eyes and return to your Sacred Space.
- Begin to write immediately.

You can start by writing something like, "Hello SOURCE! I am writing in hopes of meeting you. I would like to invite you to join me in my Sacred Space. I am feeling . . ."

Write everything about how you feel—excited, awkward, intrigued, curious, nervous, unsure—whatever comes up.

You may continue however you like, perhaps along these lines: "I would like to get to know you and to learn how you and I can have conversations. Could you let me know in some way if you are available for this first get together?"

Now here's something really important: whenever you ask a question, listen inside yourself for the answer! When it comes, write it down.

When you can't seem to get an answer, be patient. Then, when you continue, do it calmly and with an energy of acceptance.

Be completely honest! Write how you feel. If you don't know how to continue, write exactly that—that you don't know how to continue. You can always ask for help. Write, "I think I need your help. Can you tell me what you need so we can start or continue this conversation?"

Let your SOURCE know that your intention for today is simply a first meeting, and to get to know a bit more about how to best have a conversation. Asking questions is always helpful. Remember, the SOURCE is there to help you, to give you access to all the wisdom that is yours to explore.

Just let the conversation flow. Wherever it goes, it goes. Stay open and curious. We never know what is going to happen. Isn't that just wonderful?

At some point you might realize that you are too much in your head, that your brain is telling you what to write. You will be able to feel it in your head. If you realize that you are doing that, take a deep breath and redirect your attention back to your Sacred Space. Visualize the space and the SOURCE, if a visualization has already emerged. Your SOURCE may be just a voice, or a sense of a presence. Visualize (or sense) it in as much detail as possible.

When you come to the end of your time, make sure to thank the SOURCE for this first get together and, as you would with anybody you meet, say goodbye. You could write something like, "I am looking forward to meeting you again," or, "I am so happy we talked." Write whatever is true to you.

Find a way to close your session with gratitude for everything you experienced and include thanking yourself.

Continue doing this JournaLogue session until you feel that you have found a good beginning for an ongoing dialogue with your SOURCE (in any way it has revealed itself to you). This may involve journaling on this exercise for several days. When you feel that a dialogue with your SOURCE has been initiated, you are ready to move on to the next step.

Exercise V: welcoming LOVE

> "Through my love for you, I want to express my love for the whole cosmos, the whole of humanity, and all beings. By living with you, I want to learn to love everyone and all species. If I succeed in loving you, I will be able to love everyone and all species on Earth…"
> —Thich Nhat Hanh

For a fairly long time, my daily journaling practice was focused on my dialogue with my SOURCE. The conversations I documented with my Inner Wisdom never cease to amaze me. I am so grateful for the connection I have with this limitless source of wisdom, feedback, support, and even humor. I hope you are having a similar experience.

My IW is always with me, available for my questions and for dialogues. One of my most fascinating discoveries has been that as soon as I try to avoid making my own experience, with thoughts like, "I won't try, I'll just go and ask my IW," that's when my SOURCE isn't available. As long as my questions and inquiries are grounded in curiosity and a desire to find my own answers, I can always ask for help. Requests like, "Please tell me what I should do," remain unanswered every time.

Replies, if they come, are usually along the lines of, "what is it you need?" or, "what is your real question?". Only when I saw these as invitations to take ever more responsibility for my own life was I able to appreciate the immense gift of this journaling practice.

It was my IW who first invited me into a conversation with my LOVE.

In chapter 4, "The Story of Love", you read about the journey that took me to seeing love as that which connects everything, flowing through us, through other, and through all—Love As.

I invite you to sense into this story again. Sense how everything is connected to you through love. How you are connected to everything through love. Love flows through you, and it rests in you. There, where it rests in you, lies the aspect of LOVE that is uniquely yours to contribute in this life.

With that, you can turn towards the next exercise of the JournaLogue practice.

The Exercise

This exercise is about connecting to the part of you that is your LOVE and beginning your regular dialogue with it.

- Make sure you have prepared and are settled into your dedicated place.

- Have your chosen music playing (unless you prefer total silence).

- Set a timer to 30 minutes (or longer if you want).

- Open your journal and write the headline, "Welcome, LOVE!"

- Take a few deep breaths, turn your awareness inward, and visualize and enter your Sacred Space.

- Ask your SOURCE to please join you and to hold the space for you and for your LOVE.

- Close your eyes and begin sensing the connection to your LOVE. Invite it into your Sacred Space (you might even find that it is already there).

- As soon as you have the slighted sense of the presence of your LOVE, begin journaling.

Use normal phrases, like, "hello LOVE, I am so happy you are here! I would like to meet with you. Are you available?" (As always, listen carefully if there is an answer.)

Continue with your invitation, such as, "please let me invite you into my Sacred Space. I would like you to help me with my SCENARIO. I would like to learn how to shift my experience through acting from unified love and power."

Listen deeply . . . write . . .

Keep the flow of the journaling dialogue. The intention for today is to learn more about your LOVE and to find out what it needs in order to become a part of your Inner Support Team. Explore whatever is important to LOVE regarding your future dialogues and collaboration.

You might not need or want my suggestions, but in case you do, here are some questions that might help you deepen your conversation with your LOVE:

- Is there anything you want me to know about you that I haven't been able to see until now?
- Is there anything you would like to ask me?
- In which circumstances of my life can you see me expressing you the least?
- In which circumstances of my life can you see me expressing you the most?
- Is there anything I need to specifically consider in our dialogues?

These are just suggestions. Your dialogue might go in a completely different direction. Your SOURCE might have something to contribute. Maybe your SOURCE and your LOVE begin talking to each other. The practice is to stay open to it all, to allow the emergence, and to keep listening deeply and writing what you "hear".

Keep the dialogue going until your timer tells you that this JournaLogue session is coming to an end. Say thank you and goodbye to your LOVE and your SOURCE in whatever way feels suitable to you.

Once you've said goodbye, you are done with this session.

Repeat this practice until you feel that your dialogue with your LOVE is a well-integrated part of your JournaLogue practice.

You might still run into moments where a dialogue feels less comfortable, or even moments where you feel completely stuck. That is a normal part of the process. When you have some form of visualization of the part you are in dialogue with, that's a helpful sign. The visualization can be absolutely anything. A light, a shadow, a plant, an animal, a human being, or something vaguely similar to a human being, a rock, a shape, an angel, a mythical creature . . . absolutely anything. It is important that you accept whatever it is. In many cases you will find that this visualization changes over time, which is perfectly normal.

There is one important exception—if the visualization is a human being and it shows up like someone you know and who is still alive, you can be sure that it is your brain trying to take control. People who you know, or you know about, and who are still alive are not useful representations of your inner parts. If that happens, please keep looking and sensing more deeply.

With your SOURCE and your LOVE as regular visitors in your Sacred Space and with a dialogue with them emerging, you are ready to move on into the next exercise.

Exercise VI: love your POWER

> *"Authentic power is building something inside of you, which you cannot lose and that no one can take away from you."*
> —Gary Zukav

Let me begin with another dialogue from my journal:

> Me: IW and LOVE, would it be possible to listen to you two have a dialogue about what the issue for today is?
>
> *LOVE: No, that's not how it works. We need your active participation. Do you really think you can delegate your inner work to us?*
>
> Me: That makes me smile—I feel a bit like a naughty child being caught. But it's only partly that way. I was hoping that you would help me focus. I am feeling some nervousness and I just can't pin it down. I don't know where it comes from. I realize I need to ask you directly about that and not wait passively to see if it will show up. So here's my question to both of you . . .
>
> Oh WOW. While trying to formulate my question, I realized where my nervousness comes from. I can suddenly feel it very clearly: my POWER is missing in our conversation, and I am nervous about it.
>
> *IW: Yes, now you've got it. That's what is up for you next. Begin to build your relationship with your POWER and start an inner dialogue with it. Once you two have established a connection, then you, me, LOVE, and POWER can explore so many things together.*

I guess with that I have already given away that this exercise is about meeting your POWER and integrating the dialogue with it into your JournaLogue practice.

In chapter 4, "The Story of Power", you read about a new story. A story about power being that which enables everything to self-realize. A story where power is one of the gifts of spirit-consciousness-nature, that enables the manifestation of purpose, thus, to be of service to the interconnected and interdependent greater whole.

Give yourself some time to connect to and to take in this energy of POWER.

Our POWER is the energy that enables us to self-realize, to express who we are, to embody our full potential, to realize our personal purpose. Self-realization (or "Individuation" if we use Jungian terminology) is ultimately what our life is about. It is why we are here—to bring our unique gift to the world through becoming ever more of who we truly are. That is self-realization, and our POWER is what enables it.

For POWER to be an ally on our journey to self-realization, we need to be in a healthy relationship with it. Building and strengthening this relationship is one of the core aspects of the JournaLogue practice.

Before you settle down and begin with inviting your POWER into dialogue, let me share some insights from the experience of many JournaLogue practitioners.

The relationship with our POWER has a history, made up of light and shadow. This history can be burdened by POWER having felt neglected, misunderstood, or misused. Relational disturbances can be heavy in our relationship with POWER. Remember—disconnected power is at the root of all intergenerational, collective, and individual trauma.

Please be aware that in the beginning it could be difficult and even painful to connect and communicate with your POWER. You might feel challenged, and you might need a lot of patience.

As with every relationship, building a strong connection with your POWER is about building trust. This is especially true if the relationship is burdened by its history. Be clear about your intention for this part of the journey: to build a strong relationship, and to open the flow of communication with your POWER in service of your SCENARIO.

Be radically honest about your relationship with your POWER so far. Before going into dialogue, take some time to reflect on the following questions:

- What has power meant for you up to now?
- What are your beliefs about power in general and your POWER specifically?
- Where in your life do you feel powerful?
- Where in your life do you feel powerless?
- How has the power of others expressed itself in your life so far?
- How has your POWER expressed itself in your life so far?

Do you remember Marianne Williamson's quote, "our deepest fear is not that we are inadequate. Our deepest fear is that we are powerful beyond measure"? This quote invites us to talk to POWER about our fears. Often we project our fears on the outside world when we are actually afraid of fully showing our light. Try and identify the fears you have (if any!) about building a strong relationship with your POWER and explore how you can deal with those fears.

You may not be ready to open a dialogue with your POWER yet. Sometimes, it is helpful to do a few JournaLogue sessions with SOURCE and LOVE to reflect on your relationship with power in general, and your POWER specifically. Ask for their support to help you open up fully to the intention of building a healthy relationship with your POWER. Be as sure as you can that you really want to build this relationship before beginning to connect with your POWER.

When beginning your dialogue with your POWER, invite it into your Sacred Space. Speak calmly and lovingly. If you start feeling uncomfortable, give yourself time to take a few breaths, and visualize reaching out and briefly touching your LOVE. It will help you to calm down.

What we are looking to do is to "peel off" the conditioning, the beliefs, and the fears which might be in the way of us getting in contact with our authentic POWER.

Our authentic POWER is the aspect of us through which we are connected to Power As, the natural phenomenon that is there for everything. It is what enables us to self-realize, and to explore and embody ever more of our highest potential—our purpose—our soul.

The Exercise

The intention of this exercise is to set you off on your journey of getting to know, communicating with, your authentic POWER.

- Do everything you need to begin your journaling (you know: breathing, music, candles, open journal, etc.)
- Set your timer to a minimum of 35 minutes.
- Turn your awareness inward and enter your Sacred Space.
- Open your journal and write the headline, "Welcome, POWER!"
- Invite your SOURCE and your LOVE to join you and to please hold space for you and for your POWER.
- Close your eyes, and begin sensing the connection to your POWER. Invite it into your Sacred Space (you may even find that it is already there).
- As soon as you have the slightest sense of the presence of your POWER, begin journaling.

Let it flow . . . be available for everything, even for nothing. Just keep writing. If it takes time, that's fine. If not today, then perhaps tomorrow the dialogue can begin. It really depends on the relationship you have had so far with your POWER, and by that, I mean your authentic POWER—not the story of power we all have been told and taught to believe. Maybe you are already well acquainted with your authentic POWER, or maybe not. If not, it might be a while before a conversation becomes possible. Remember that you can always turn to both your SOURCE and your LOVE for support.

Whatever happens in this session in your Sacred Space, put it in writing.

When the timer tells you that you are at the end, do one more thing: write a message of gratitude. Tell your POWER what you are grateful for this JournaLogue session. If you need two or more sessions to reach a flowing dialogue with your POWER, close with gratitude every time. Even if POWER hasn't communicated with you yet, I assure you it can hear you.

Please remember to end the session not just with POWER, but also with your SOURCE and your LOVE. Thank them and say goodbye to them as well.

As soon as you have a sense that you have begun a dialogue with your POWER, you are ready to move on to the next exercise.

Exercise VII: the welcome ritual

> "Empty but always full -
> welcome home to your true self."
> —Unknown

This and the next exercise will give you opportunities to deepen your JournaLogue practices of communicating with your SOURCE, LOVE and POWER. They will also help you enjoy your time in your Sacred Space, which I'm sure is a beautiful, unique, and nourishing place for you to visit with your Inner Support Team.

Before we invite others into this unique space, I want to introduce you to an important practice that will help you to be even better prepared for your JournaLogue sessions.

This practice will help you to be fully present and ready for dialogue each time you begin journaling. Experience has shown that sometimes this can be hard. Sometimes things worry us, put us under time pressure, or distract us in some other way. What happens then is that we often sit and start thinking, "what should I write?" Sometimes we are so distracted by thoughts, by the "monkey chatter" in our brain, and it all gets in the way of us starting the JournaLogue.

This practice is the "Welcome Ritual".

The Welcome Ritual supports two things. First, it lets you invite yourself to fully arrive in your Sacred Space. At the same time, it brings you into deeper contact with the flow of the journaling practice. It is a ritual that will help you let go of any distractions and begin writing.

Once your Welcome Ritual has become a regular practice for you, you'll experience another benefit in addition to easier daily journaling. Once you memorize the ritual, it will help you access your Sacred Space for a dialogue with any of your inner parts, no matter where you are and no matter what is happening around you. You'll have this new capacity not just during your JournaLogue practice, but any time you need access to your inner resources.

Like most of the practices of the JournaLogue, the Welcome Ritual emerged from a dialogue with my IW. I had been struggling with focusing and beginning to journal, even though I had settled into my dedicated space, meditated, turned on my usual music, and so forth. These steps are, in themselves, already a ritual, but it turned out that something additional was needed. Once I found my specific Welcome Ritual, it helped me a great deal to arrive in my Sacred Space and to bring presence and mindfulness to my various dialogues.

I began by writing some greeting words. The first phrasing of my Welcome Ritual was, "good morning! I am inviting myself into my inner space of peace and connectedness. Welcome!" As the JournaLogue practices emerged, I wasn't alone anymore and my inner space became my Sacred Space. The Welcome Ritual changed and went through a few iterations.

Today I begin by folding my hands and bowing, and then I write, "good morning! I am welcoming all of us in this Sacred Space." For now, this feels wonderful to me. I assume that it will continue to change in the future, but I don't think about that. Evolutions will unfold naturally. No matter what the Welcome Ritual consists of and how it changes over time, I always begin with it once I have settled in to start the practice.

Your ritual will likely be different from mine. It is not about finding a perfect form. Writing a phrase or a sentence or two is an important part of the ritual, as it helps you to get into journaling mode, but what you write and what else you might do as part of the ritual is entirely up to you. Just let it emerge. It will support you in arriving in your Sacred Space with presence and in beginning your dialogues.

It is essential to the ritual that you write your phrase over and over again, repeating until the visualization and the full sense of your Sacred Space with all its "guests" has built up. You will develop a very good sense of that moment over time.

In the beginning you might need to write the sentence six or seven times, but soon it will decrease. The need for repetition may vary from day to day. Some days we are more distracted, and some days less. I only bow once at the beginning of the ritual, and normally I write my phrase twice. On other days, I do need to repeat it four or five times until I feel I have really arrived in my Sacred Space and am ready to move on.

Important: Do your Welcome Ritual every single time you begin journaling!

As mentioned before, you might find that your welcome sentence changes over time, which in itself is a lovely experience.

The Exercise

From now on you won't be reminded about how to settle in for your JournaLogue session. By now, I assume this has turned into a habit and evolved to reflect your own personal style.

- Set your timer to a minimum of 25 minutes and open your journal.
- Write the headline, "My Welcome Ritual".

Your Welcome Ritual might already be clear to you after reading the exercise introduction above, or you might want to experiment a bit. Take your time to find a phrase, or one or two sentences. What else might be part of your ritual? Allow the emergence of something that brings the sense of fully arriving in your Sacred Space.

Please remember, all you need is a first version. Your Welcome Ritual will evolve as you continue the JournaLogue practice.

Once you feel you have found the first version of your Welcome Ritual, turn your inner attention to your entire Sacred Space. In case they haven't arrived already, one after the other invite your SOURCE, your LOVE, and your POWER to come and join you. Invite each to choose their place. Welcome each of them individually, and when they are all settled, address all of them and ask them for input. You can say something like, "I would like to ask you all—is there anything else I need to be aware of, or need to consider, so we can repeatedly gather here for our dialogues in support of my SCENARIO?"

Listen deeply . . . write . . . ask (and write) more questions if something comes up. Let it flow.

When the timer rings, finish what you are writing and find a suitable way to thank your Inner Support Team. Say goodbye.

When you feel comfortable with your Welcome Ritual and also feel that the gatherings with all three members of your Inner Support Team are going well, then you are ready to move on to the next exercise.

Exercise VIII: yay for the small things!

> "When life gets difficult then we realize the importance of small things."
> —Ishan Ahuja

Can you remember the story of my client Bettina and her experience in the Pharmacy? This story describes a situation similar to what so many of us encounter again and again. Things large or small can trigger us in different ways, causing us to feel frustrated, angry, hurt, misunderstood, or let down. We're all familiar with these unpleasant feelings and emotions.

The JournaLogue practice, like other practices of self-reflection and introspection, can help us to see that these triggers always are rooted in our shadows, and that life will continue to present us with these triggers as ongoing opportunities to learn ever more about ourselves.

These opportunities show up in different forms and sizes. Don't miss out on the learning opportunities that these situations offer. The journaling practice has taught its practitioners over and over again: *start looking for the small things!*

Before I learned to understand and integrate this, I had already been doing a lot of reflection and introspection, trying to learn through and from my shadows. My tendency was to look at the big life issues that I felt would be hard to deal with. Through the JournaLogue practice this changed. I discovered an important aspect of this practice: many small things add up, and potentially lead to big shifts.

At this point the practice is about looking for small, everyday things that we experience as unpleasant and that trigger us. We are looking for small experiments, small opportunities to practice. This is almost like training to build muscle. This practice will enable you to eventually turn to your SCENARIO and other significant situations, relationships, and issues in life.

We experience way more of these incidents in our everyday life than we tend to be aware of. We have learned to accept many little disturbances as part of life—and while it might be true that such disturbances are unavoidable, that doesn't mean that we can't work with them to support our learning. Greater wellbeing is possible when we learn to consciously shift our unpleasant experiences into something that feels better for us.

Behind each of these triggers lies an opportunity to learn. Now that you have an Inner Support Team from which you can ask for help, you can access unlimited support for this learning process. Your SOURCE, LOVE, and POWER have so much information for you, and they can help you develop practices to detect and benefit from these learning opportunities.

In preparation for the upcoming exercise, you need to first identify what in the JournaLogue practice is called a "signal". Identifying your signal will help you become aware of little learning opportunities—those chances to practice shifting how you feel and act in a situation you initially experience as unpleasant.

Please remember a recent, small situation where you felt triggered. Perhaps someone didn't do something you felt you had the right to expect, or someone was unpunctual and kept you waiting . . . again. Maybe someone didn't greet you, and you felt the person had intentionally looked away. Those are all fairly normal everyday things that happen. This exercise is called "yay for the small things", so please choose a situation that triggered you, but that isn't too serious—we don't want it to stand for what to you is a really big life issue.

Continue to read when you've identified a situation.

Now close your eyes. Remember the situation. Where were you? Who else was involved? What did you and/or others say? Recall your internal reaction. How did it make you feel, emotionally? Were you angry? Frustrated? Hurt? Let down? Not heard?

Ask yourself, "where in your body can you locate this emotion?" Place your hand over that location in your body to identify it even more.

Every emotion expresses itself through a physical sensation. The physical sensation is your signal. We all have it, but sometimes we are quite used to pushing it away or simply ignoring it. While you still have your hand over the location of your signal, describe to yourself in more detail how the sensation feels.

To give you an example, my signal is a feeling of tightening in my throat, as if something were stuck. Do you know the feeling when you swallow a really big pill, and even though you drank plenty of water, it still feels as if it were stuck in your throat? That's what my signal feels like.

What does your signal feel like?

Continue to read when you have identified and described your signal. If you feel like it, write that description into your journal.

Now, if you can, give your signal a name. Mine is called "lump", which enables me to acknowledge it in a short way. So, instead of thinking, "here's that feeling that I get when I'm swallowing a really big pill and it gets stuck in my throat," I simply recognize, "here's lump again".

When I first experimented with this practice, I found out that I had ignored my signal for a very long time. In fact, I am not sure if I had actually ever been clearly aware of it before I experimented with this practice. It did take me a while to be able to really identify it, but now I am immensely thankful for it. My signal always helps me to become aware of what is really going on for me in the present moment, instead of being stuck in my frustration, anger, or hurt. I now know that "lump" is important and useful because it points me towards something that I can address and treat as a learning opportunity.

The Exercise

This exercise is about learning to shift your experience of situations that trigger you with the help of your LOVE and POWER. I suggest you set your timer to 40 minutes, as it will require a bit more time. Also, you may need a few sessions to finish this exercise. It is important that you give it all the time it needs, as it is a pivotal point of the process.

- Settle into your dedicated space.
- Set your timer.
- Open your journal and do your Welcome Ritual.
- Write the headline, "Starting with Small Things."
- Start journaling immediately.

See if all members of your Inner Support Team are present. If not, connect to each of them and invite them to join you in your Sacred Space. Wait until all are settled in.

Now ask your SOURCE to please hold space for your dialogue with your LOVE and POWER. Then, turn to LOVE and POWER and begin by talking about your SCENARIO. Clarify that you are seeking support in developing some practices to help you prepare for it.

Tell them about the signal you have identified.

Turn to LOVE and begin a dialogue. One way to deepen the connection is to talk about any questions you might have about the Web of Love. This can deepen your sense of interconnectedness and interdependence with everything through your LOVE. You might visualize sitting closer to LOVE, maybe even holding hands, or embracing one another. Let the sense of deeper connection emerge in its own way.

Ask your LOVE to help you develop a practice that will support you in shifting your reaction once you have become aware of your signal, thus identifying a learning opportunity. If you have given the signal a name, use it in your dialogues. Explore together what you can do once you are aware of your signal. You may ask questions like:

- How can the awareness of this signal help me to deliberately connect to you, LOVE, in this moment?

- What practice can bring me back into deeper connection, into increased resonance with the Web of Love, with Love AS, so that I can then act from this deep connection with you, LOVE?

As always, listen deeply and keep journaling.

Exploring answers to your questions is never about "getting it right" or "finding the perfect answer". This is about going into your first experiments of the JournaLogue practice. You will try things out, seeing if what comes up for you is helpful and noticing what doesn't feel useful. Bring your experience back into further dialogues with LOVE.

When you feel that a first idea of what you could try has emerged and you feel that you can move on, thank LOVE, and turn to your POWER.

Repeat the same process with your POWER.

Begin by deepening the sense of connection with your POWER, and through it, with Power As. You can visualize moving closer to POWER, maybe holding hands, or even embracing. Let the sense of deepened connection emerge in its own way.

Then explore with your POWER how it can help you shift your experience once you are aware of your signal. Ask similar questions to those you asked LOVE. For example:

- How can the awareness of this signal help me to deliberately connect to you, POWER, at this moment?
- What practice can bring me back into deeper connection, into increased resonance with you and Power AS, so that I can then act from this deep connection with my authentic POWER?
- How can my reaction to the signal shift, when I am deeply connected to you, POWER, and to LOVE at the same time?

If POWER and LOVE begin talking to each other, simply keep listening and journaling the dialogue.

New Stories of Love, Power, and Purpose

When the timer tells you that it's time to wrap up—and unless you want to go on—thank LOVE, POWER, and SOURCE for this session. It might be useful to express the intention to continue this conversation in your next session.

Find a suitable way to say goodbye and close the session for this time.

As I mentioned before, it might take a few sessions before you develop a good sense of a practice that can help you in shifting an experience where you feel triggered into a situation that you experience as loving and powerful—even in small things.

Joanna, a UK based participant in a JournaLogue program, described her experience of this step like this:

> *"It took me about five or six JournaLogue sessions, and some experimenting, until my practice shaped up for me. What emerged was a sequence of small movements. First, I close my eyes (just a few seconds), straighten my back, take a deep breath, and lightly put my fingertips to the area of my body where my signal is located. This immediately connects me to my LOVE. Simultaneously, in my imagination I can see a very colorful picture that I drew when initially exploring this step with my POWER. I have the picture in my home, and I took a photo of it with my mobile to have it available there for a while, but by now I don't need to look at it anymore. The picture shows up in my mind's eye while I do my little movements and that helps me tune back into higher resonance with LOVE and POWER. The whole practice only takes a few seconds, and it enables me to deal with a triggering situation in a completely different way."*

Joanna then went on to describe an experiment she did. Like in Bettina's story, it was a commonplace situation that first gave her the sense of the deep potential of this practice.

> *"I work in a dental clinic, where I am in charge of finances. We had a new team member. Soon after she began, I observed that every once in a while she arrived late at work. Not dramatically late, but 10 to 15 minutes. I asked her about it, and whether there was something that*

was in her way of coming to work punctually. She apologized and said that it happened because she had a really long commute, and the connections sometimes were bad. I asked her to please do her best to be punctual, as it is often in the morning that I need to collect specific information from the team members."

"To me, punctuality is very important and an expression of reliability. I really get triggered by people who are unpunctual and let me wait. Soon after our conversation I was under time pressure with finalizing some work and needed information from Mariah in the morning. You can guess—she wasn't there again. My initial reaction was anger and frustration, not just because of her being unpunctual again, but also because I felt disrespected as her boss. My first thoughts were about having a serious conversation with her, telling her that I would give her one more chance to prove that she was reliable, and other unpleasant thoughts."

"Then I remembered that what I was experiencing was a signal that pointed me towards a learning opportunity. I did my practice, and I could immediately feel how my mood shifted from anger to curiosity and compassion. I realized that judging Mariah as unpunctual, unreliable, and disrespectful had completely disconnected me from my ability to be curious about what was really happening and compassionate for what might be going on for another person."

"I could now address Mariah in a way that led to a very touching conversation. I learned that a very difficult family situation led to her coming late, and that she had felt too ashamed to talk about it. We discussed how we could make things work together, and in the end it was no problem at all. Since then, Mariah and I have gotten along very well. Working together is a great pleasure and one of her best qualities is that she is super reliable."

"I learned many things from this experience—most importantly, that our habitual reactions, our patterns, have the power to completely rob us of the ability to be present and aware of what is really going on in any given moment."

In this exercise, give yourself time to let your individual practice emerge. Experiment with your signal and the individual practice that follows it in your everyday life and bring your experiences back into your JournaLogue sessions. Once you feel that you have increased your capacity to become aware of even small triggers and your signal, and to intentionally react by doing your practice to reconnect with LOVE and POWER, then you are ready to move on to the next exercise.

Exercise IX: befriending your SABOTEUR

> "All the beauty of life
> is made up
> of light and shadow."
> —Leo Tolstoy

By now you have established communications with the first three members of your Inner Support Team: your SOURCE, LOVE, and POWER. You can count on this team to help you begin the next phase of your JournaLogue. They are, and will be, with you—every step of the way, for as long as you invite them.

With this exercise we are beginning to explore what exactly it is when we are holding back from doing what we want to do—when something comes up (fear, doubt, reasoning) and we decide against our intuition.

Before you read on, please choose one thing in your life that you have been wanting to do for a while, but for whatever reason just hasn't happened. For example, have you been wanting to clarify something with someone—a friend, colleague, boss, partner, child, or neighbor—but are afraid of how this person will react? Do you want to leave your job, but don't believe you will find a new job that you will like more, or have another reason for not acting? Have you wanted to play a musical instrument, draw, paint, sing, dance, write, or do something else creative, but don't believe you have enough talent or time? Have you been too busy or too stressed for too long, and though you really don't want that any more you don't know how to change it? Maybe you would love to climb Mt. Kilimanjaro, but don't believe you can do it?

This last example is personal for me. I always liked hiking in the mountains, but I never actually felt drawn to summit a high peak until I visited Kenya. I was taken to a viewpoint from which I could watch the sun set behind Mt. Kilimanjaro. This gave rise to an incredible yearning. I wanted to befriend this beautiful being through hiking to the top.

For some years, I told myself that I was crazy. I was not an athlete, and I would never be able to do that! But what do you know—at the age of 57, I summited Mt. Kilimanjaro! It was a deeply spiritual experience for which I am endlessly grateful.

It's important to note that opting out of certain experiences or choices is just fine. Not every decision "against" means missing out on something, but we are at our best when we can make decisions with full awareness, not from unconscious patterns. This capacity opens up new possibilities in life.

Have you identified something in your life that you have been wanting to do for a while, but for whatever reason it just hasn't happened yet? It doesn't have to be a big mountain (in the metaphorical sense). It might be something that has come up recently, no matter how small it might feel now. Visualize, in fine detail, a situation where your issue occurs. If you wish to, you may write about this situation and how you experience it in your journal.

Once you have decided with which situation or issue you will explore further into the next exercise, you are ready to read on.

Whenever we feel that something is holding us back, we are experiencing the sabotaging pattern of a part inside of us. This part exposes fears that cause us to make choices that block our own authentic power and love and limit us in living our highest potential. It acts from the shadow, from the unconscious, which is why it can be difficult for us to detect, to explore, and ultimately to shift its patterns.

Like all of our parts, this one has a shadow side, but it also has a wonderful, light side. This exercise has two parts. We will first explore the shadow side, then explore the light side of this part.

This inner part originally formed for a very good reason. At some point in our lives, we needed to develop a behavior as part of our survival strategy. Caroline Myss has identified a group of these patterns as "Archetypes of Survival"[31]. At this point in our JournaLogue journey, we are addressing one of these Archetypes—the Saboteur. If our heart is yearning for something, but we keep choosing to act in a way that won't allow us to follow this yearning, that's when our actions are guided by our SABOTEUR and its patterns.

Starting early in our lives, the SABOTEUR protects us from doing things that could cause us pain—whether it be punishment, rejection, ridicule, deprivation of love, or some other consequence. This was not just useful, but necessary for us to navigate our relationships with the people we depended on. For most of us, as we grow older, the initial reason for our SABOTEUR to protect us doesn't exist anymore. Our Saboteur isn't aware of that. Our formed pattern keeps guiding our behaviors in the same way over and over again, driving us on autopilot, keeping us doing things that are not in alignment with our authentic potential.

It is a powerful process to explore our archetypal shadow patterns and to transcend and include them in our life in a new way. You can find a lot of useful information on the Saboteur Archetype from various teachers. Much of the JournaLogue practices around the Saboteur are based on the work of Caroline Myss and Stacey Couch[32].

---

[31] For deeper insights into archetypes read: Caroline Myss, Sacred Contracts; (Bantam; 1st UK Paperback Edition (5 Aug. 2002)); Archetypes: A Beginner's Guide to Your Inner-net; Also find free resources on Caroline Myss' Website: https://www.myss.com

[32] Stacey Couch works closely with Caroline Myss and offers great programs to learn more about Archetypes and the Archetypes of Survival in particular: https://www.wildgratitude.com/product-category/online-classes/

There are two general patterns in which the shadow of the Saboteur tends to show up. One way lets us create too much change in our lives. When we are constantly looking for a way out, we rarely arrive to rest and enjoy. The second pattern is that we allow too little or no change in our lives. This leads us to complaining that we feel stuck, and we can't see a way out.

The Saboteur uses a selection of strategies to express either of those general patterns, and we can detect these strategies in recognizable and observable behaviors. While you read through these strategies and their respective behaviors, try and sense what rings true for you. Relate back to the situation or issue you identified above and try to be honest. Ask yourself, "which of the following behaviors do I know in myself, and which ones relate specifically to the situation I have identified?" It's quite possible that a few of these behaviors will resonate with you.

- **Too many options:** you are rarely content with a situation for a long period of time and have too many plans running at the same time.

- **Disruption or distraction:** you give in to all kinds of distractions (conversations with friends and colleagues, getting tea or coffee, always being reachable by phone, emails, social media) and tend to jump from thing to thing to thing. This can look like not completing projects and taking on many projects at the same time.

- **Resisting change:** change is frightening to you, so you choose unconsciously to do nothing or to stick with the status quo.

- **Procrastination or laziness:** you slow down change by putting things off. This can look like deferring your dreams, getting stuck in a "when/then" thought pattern, putting off your priorities, de-prioritizing things that would help you get into a better place, or secretly hoping that things will change without you having to do anything.

- **Excuses:** your arguments are mainly, "I don't have a choice," and, "I can't because . . .", "that won't work because . . .", or "others won't accept that because . . .".

- **Drama:** you tend to make a big deal out of things, often blowing them out of proportion. You invite everyone's opinion and keep telling the story of how this isn't working, over and over and over again. You spend a lot of time talking about a change, a decision, or choice, yet not actually doing anything about it. You make a big deal out of the matter, while stretching it out much longer than necessary.

- **Doubt:** you constantly question a path once you have chosen it. You repeatedly undermine yourself, your cause, your path, and your empowerment.

As you read through the description of these behaviors, did you recognize which ones show up in your life? Did you recognize which ones show up in the specific situation or issue you identified for the upcoming exercise?

Please take your time to do that. Identify which one (or more) of these behaviors seem familiar to you, and those that show up in the issue you identified. Take the above behavior descriptions and translate them into your situation, describing which of your behavior(s) is or are in the way of you getting what you desire.

John, one of my clients in the U.S., shared what he experienced at this part of the JournaLogue. He had identified this dream, this deep desire of his, to be able to sing. He couldn't quite understand how this came up, because he knew that he couldn't sing, that he couldn't hold a tune, and that he didn't have a nice voice. He wrote:

"I never realized how much I was behaving on "autopilot" in connection with this wish of mine, that I had been holding for so many years, and that always seemed completely unfulfillable to me.

As a small child, perhaps two or three years of age, I used to sing a lot. From what my mother told me, it wasn't singing in the "normal" sense, like singing children's songs or other tunes I might have heard and memorized. I made up my own tunes, and to my parents they were uncomfortable to listen to and a disturbance. They told me to stop doing that, and after a while I did. In a recent conversation with my mother, I found out that there was never any music in our home. It just wasn't something my parents enjoyed.

When I came to this part of the JournaLogue, I realized that I had been holding a deep desire which expressed itself every time I heard someone sing. I am a huge fan of Italian operas, and I can't get enough of listening to the Three Tenors. Every time I listened, an inner voice called out, "how I wish I could sing like that!" This was immediately followed by another voice, saying, "don't be ridiculous! You don't sing, you make noise when you try. Remember—it's noise that disturbs others.

Through the dialogue with my SABOTEUR, I found out that my need "not to disturb others" had not just stopped me from singing but had grown to influence many aspects of my life. I could suddenly see how, in many different situations, I had felt like doing something but had made excuses why I couldn't—that it would be inconsiderate of others, a disturbance, and therefore a selfish thing to do.

In dialogue with my SABOTEUR, I learned how it had helped me be considerate of others, and how this was one of my qualities that my loved ones, friends, and colleagues appreciate greatly. I also learned that I know very well how to be considerate of others, but I don't know how to be considerate of myself. I began to see that being considerate of self and others wasn't an "either/or" but a "both/and" situation.

Over time this realization shifted many things in my life for the better, but first and foremost it shifted my approach to singing. I joined a community that gathered regularly to chant together. Chanting gave me many gifts, including a completely new relationship with my voice. This brought with it a completely new way of "speaking my voice"—with love and power—when singing, and otherwise."

The intention of Part 1 of the upcoming exercise is for you to connect to your SABOTEUR and to invite it to join your Inner Support Team in your Sacred Space.

To give you an example, here's a part of my journal. This dialogue followed a few intense sessions with my IW, which finally led me to understand the need to connect to and befriend my SABOTEUR.

SABOTEUR: Why do you want to talk to me?

ME: Until today I have only seen one part of you and have always judged the way you made me feel. I saw you as something bad that I wanted to get rid of. But the conversation with my IW made me see how important you are, and that there is more to you.

SABOTEUR: I don't trust you. I feel you are only repeating what your Inner Wisdom told you.

ME: I am very insecure about talking to you. I feel I don't know you, and to be honest I don't really trust you either. You have caused me so much pain.

SABOTEUR: I don't understand—I have always been trying to take care of you and to protect you from pain.

ME: I really want to believe you, but I am struggling. How can we get into a dialogue in which we can get to know each other better? I want to trust you.

SABOTEUR: I want to trust you as well.

ME: Let me begin by saying thank you for being here, and willing to talk to me. Also, I am really sorry about how I judged and blamed you!

SABOTEUR: That feels nice. Thank you for saying this and I believe you. Please believe me that I never ever intended to hurt you. All I ever want to do is protect you. I remember how well that worked. I know you needed me—and then I began to feel like you were trying to get rid of me, no matter how hard I tried to show you that you needed me.

ME: This must have been when I repeatedly realized that something was holding me back from what I really wanted to do or say. I want to learn so much more about you.

SABOTEUR: Really?

ME: Yes, I'm honest! Please, can we continue talking about this? Maybe we can find a way to become friends.

SABOTEUR: Ok, yes, let's try that. I would like that, and to be honest, it would make life so much easier for both of us.

It is time to step into the actual exercise.

The Exercise (Part 1)

- Make yourself comfortable in your dedicated space and do everything you normally do to get started.
- Set your timer for the time you are giving yourself for today's assignment. My suggestion is 40 minutes.
- Open your journal and put the headline, "Befriending my SABOTEUR"
- Begin the visualization and journaling exercise described below.

Connect to the situation or issue you identified where you acted in one way but would have liked to have acted differently. Go into that memory in as much detail as you can. Try and identify the moment where you decided to do one thing, while your authentic reaction would have been to do something else.

Close your eyes and connect to your SOURCE, LOVE, and POWER in your Sacred Space. Invite them to hold space for you while you are going through this exercise.

When you and your Inner Support Team are all settled in, tell them (keep journaling!) everything about your internal experiences while reading the information leading up to this exercise. Which behavior pattern(s) did you identify with? When does this pattern show up, either in your recent life or even further back? What strategies keep you from fulfilling your desires? How does it feel to be dealing with this pattern?

Stay honest with yourself—nobody's looking over your shoulder or listening. And remember—where there is shadow, there is light. We will explore the light next.

If nothing flows immediately, here are some questions that can help:

- How did it feel to identify my behavior patterns in this way?
- How do the strategies I identified show up in my behavior in the issue or situation I chose?
- What else came to my mind while exploring what was holding me back in my identified issue or situation?

Try and capture this within the first 10 minutes of your session. Once you feel you have captured what is important about your experience, stop writing briefly and take a few deep breaths. It is important that you remain in your Sacred Space with your awareness.

Let your breath return to its normal rhythm, and then continue writing. Begin addressing your SABOTEUR. Here's a suggestion for how you can begin:

"SABOTEUR, I have seen that you are playing an important role in my life and that I haven't paid much attention to what you are intending to do for me. I would like to invite you to join my Inner Support Team so we can dialogue about this. I want to get to know you better."

Keep writing whatever it is that you are internally hearing, seeing, and feeling. Don't stop writing to think things over.

Once you get a sense that your SABOTEUR is present, continue to address it directly. Be aware that there might be some difficult history between you. Be sensitive to your SABOTEUR'S needs, and to your own needs. Focus on building a relationship, and don't yet try to talk about the issue or situation you want to explore.

If your SOURCE, LOVE, or POWER want to contribute to the conversation, listen carefully to what they have to say. If you reach a point where you don't know what else to say to your SABOTEUR and the conversation feels stuck, you can always ask your Inner Support Team members for help.

Keep journaling everything.

The aim at this point is to invite your SABOTEUR to join you in your Sacred Space and to become a part of your Inner Support Team. Be clear about your intention of wanting to get to know it better, thereby getting to know yourself better. Let your SABOTEUR know that you are looking to build this relationship so that you can learn to appreciate it fully.

When your timer tells you that it is time to wrap up, find a good way to say goodbye to your SABOTEUR. Thank it, so that in your next conversation you can continue where you are leaving off today.

Before you close this session, thank your SOURCE, LOVE, and POWER for holding space and for their contributions, if there were any.

Then it's time to close the session.

If dealing with your SABOTEUR is completely new to you, it might take a few sessions until the dialogue can begin to flow.

No matter how many sessions you need, make sure you've reached the point where your SABOTEUR is willing to join your sessions in your Sacred Space as a member of your Inner Support Team and to be in dialogue with you. Then you can move on to Part 2.

In Part 1 of this exercise, we explored how our SABOTEUR can keep us stuck in a pattern, a habitual way of acting, instead of allowing us to act from presence, intuition, and creativity and consequently expressing our authentic self.

The habitual pattern leads us to be disempowered, which means we are disconnected from our POWER. It also leaves us with negative feelings based on fears, coming from the sense of "even though I would love to, I can't because":

- I fear that others will laugh at me, will think I'm crazy, will judge me for being selfish, will think badly of me in another way, or just won't like me anymore.
- I fear losing my job, my home, my relationship, my friends, or something else important to me.
- I fear not being able to support myself or having to depend on others in any way.
- I have difficult feelings rooted in fears of not getting my core needs met.

These disabling fears are anchored in a sense that showing our true self isn't "good" enough and are therefore anchored in low self-esteem. Self-esteem results from self-love, which means that better self-esteem—and a shift in these fear-based stories—can be achieved through being fully connected to our LOVE.

By now we already know so much about our SABOTEUR. We can see

- That it entered our life in support of our survival strategies.
- That it kept doing what it originally entered our life to do, with the ongoing intention to help us.
- That for the most part it was stuck in our shadow, and therefore mostly ignored.
- That it was met with our judgment and contempt because of what it did.

What might become possible if we invite our SABOTEUR out of the shadow into the light?

With Part 1 of this exercise, we have already begun to invite our SABOTEUR into the light, which means into our awareness. And we have invited it into dialogue. Being aware of a pattern gives us the opportunity to change it. We now can explore together with our SABOTEUR whether there is a way to behave differently, while still making sure our core needs are met.

This awareness will allow you to recognize when your SABOTEUR shows up. You already know how to recognize similar inner processes, as you have identified your signal. When our SABOTEUR shows up, we recognize this through a signal as well.

It might feel the same, or it might be a different signal. Please connect back to the situation you are working with in these exercises, the one where you are holding back. I asked you earlier to try and find out exactly when, in this situation, you make the decision to *not* do what your heart is longing for but instead to follow the habitual behavior, the pattern. At this point there is always a signal. In the past, this signal has activated your habitual behavior or pattern. It is at this exact moment that your SABOTEUR offers you a choice.

We can change our perspective on the SABOTEUR, change the story we are holding about our SABOTEUR, and decide to see its different side—the light side. We can change a behavior pattern when we understand that *the signal we feel when the SABOTEUR shows up* and *the way we react to it* are two different things.

We have a choice in the way we react.

We can see that our SABOTEUR is our "Guardian of Choice". It calls our attention to situations in which we are in danger of sabotaging ourselves, and even when we are in danger of being sabotaged. This happens when we allow the behavior of others to stop us from following our yearning.

The Saboteur's "call to attention" is also a trigger, and we feel the signal. This signal enables us to become aware. It shows us that now we have a choice about how we want to react.

Seeing and understanding this light side of our SABOTEUR can enable us to step out of our habitual reaction. Seeing and understanding this will enable us to befriend our SABOTEUR, which will help us to change the specific patterns that keep us from embodying our authentic self and manifesting our purpose.

With this, you can now move to the next exercise.

The Exercise (Part 2)

- Set the conditions for your practice and settle into your space.
- Set your timer to anything between 30 and 45 minutes. I suggest you give yourself the maximum time you can dedicate, in this range.
- Open your journal and put the headline, "Befriending my Saboteur, Part 2".
- Close your eyes and one after the other connect to and greet your SOURCE, LOVE, POWER, and your SABOTEUR.
- When you are all settled in, start journaling immediately.

Take another deep breath and seek to connect even more with your SABOTEUR. You can address it, visualize that you go and sit closer to it, or do anything else that makes clear that you are looking to begin today's dialogue with it.

Keep the intention in your mind and heart: to continue building relationship and trust with your SABOTEUR, as a member of your Inner Support Team. Share your intention. Let your SABOTEUR know why this dialogue, and your relationship, is so important to you.

Together, explore the old habitual pattern, the moment of choice. You might discuss possible new behaviors to experiment with, or anything else that comes up.

Please make sure this is a dialogue! Our parts need to be heard, and they need to feel that we are honestly interested—that we are trying to understand their perspective, and to learn from them. My

Saboteur told me its name, which helped me a lot in building the relationship.

Let it flow.

When the timer tells you that the time is over, find an appropriate way of closing today's dialogue, including saying thank you and goodbye.

If you feel it is useful, repeat the sessions to befriend your SABOTEUR. Do this until you have developed a sense of your SABOTEUR as your "Guardian of Choice" and the value this perspective can bring to your decisions, supporting ways to act that are true to you.

With this you are ready to move on in your JournaLogue journey.

Exercise X: support, support, support

> *"I was always looking outside myself
> for strength and confidence,
> but it comes from within.
> It is there all the time."*
> —Anna Freud

With the ability to invite your SOURCE, LOVE, POWER, and SABOTEUR into your Sacred Space and into dialogue, your core Inner Support Team is complete. As you continue with the JournaLogue practice, other parts of you may show up. They may join for one or more sessions and leave again, or they may become additional core Inner Support Team members. I have mentioned some of the parts that have shown up for me, such as my CREATIVITY.

As I have no way of knowing which additional parts might show up for you in the course of this JournaLogue, the exercises will continue to focus on the current core members. Nonetheless, when an additional part shows up for you, please make sure to address and integrate that part in your Sacred Space and in your dialogues in whatever way you feel is needed. You can trust that you will receive all the information you need.

This exercise is focused on further developing your collaboration with your Inner Support Team. So far, the exercises have focused primarily on one or two members, to build relationships and to invite and include the parts of your Inner Support Team. With this exercise, you are turning every JournaLogue session into a full Inner Support Team gathering. To do that, you need to know a few important things about the process.

- I am using "gathering" as a generic term. You might want to find your own suitable word to describe the occasions when you gather with your Inner Support Team to get input on how to shift into acting from unified love and power in service to purpose.

- The JournaLogue is a contemplative practice. When your mind goes wandering and all sorts of thoughts begin to swirl around your head, acknowledge them and let them go by like waves in the ocean. Come back to where you are in your journaling and continue.

When that happens to me, I always continue writing relentlessly, documenting everything. For example, "wait, I just realized my head is swirling with all sorts of thoughts. I am distracted and can't focus on what you, IW, are telling me. Let me take a deep breath to come back with my attention. Ok, I'm back. Can you please repeat what you last said?" When I go back and read my journal, I find many sentences like this.

Having said all that, we can now turn towards the steps for you to hold your first full Inner Support Team Gathering.

The Exercise

- Get settled.
- Set your timer to anything from 30 and 45 minutes, depending on how much time you want to give yourself.
- Open your journal and write the headline, "Our First Inner Support Team Gathering".
- Begin journaling immediately.

Connect to each member by directing your internal attention to them, one after the other. Greet and invite each of them individually to the gathering.

When all have joined, you can continue.

Inform all members about the intention of this gathering: to mutually define a form for the gatherings of this team, so it meets each member's needs (including yours!).

Let all members know how you feel and be honest about your hopes and fears (only regarding the gatherings, not yet about the general issue of your SCENARIO).

Address each member individually and ask, "Is there anything you need from me so you can fully participate in this and future gatherings?"

Then, ask if any of the members want to say something to another member besides you—and listen deeply to any conversation that might emerge. Don't stop writing, no matter how deeply you are listening.

If you still have time, you can invite a closing round, where each member, one after the other (including you!), speaks about the gathering or anything else that needs to be said. Be aware that if you begin this round, you need to give time for all members to speak, even if the timer signals that your time is up.

When the timer tells you it is time to close, or when the closing round is finished, close the gathering as you normally do.

After closing, turn your awareness toward yourself in the surroundings of your dedicated JournaLogue space and take a few seconds of silence and breathing.

Then ask yourself the following question. Write the question, and the answer, into your journal. "What is the most important thing I learned about my Inner Support Team in this gathering?"

I have one more suggestion: thank yourself for the wonderful attention you are giving yourself! When I do this, I actually pat my shoulder and speak out loud. "Well done and thank you, Christiane!" It feels good.

Now you are done with this JournaLogue exercise.

Don't hesitate to repeat this gathering if you feel you still need more information from any, or all, Inner Support Team members about the future gatherings. Gift yourself with high awareness of the level of comfort and joy that you sense when looking forward to the upcoming gatherings. Any sense of being anxious, insecure, or otherwise held back from doing the JournaLogue gatherings and dialogues is something that wants and needs attention. Repeat this exercise in varying ways, turning to your inner voices for help to overcome and integrate any possible inhibitions.

Setting your expectations too high and wanting to move on fast with the practice might be an old pattern of your SABOTEUR. Doubting your ability to build a really strong relationship with any one of your parts might be grounded in disconnection from your self-love. Doubting your ability to actually go through with your SCENARIO could come from poor connection to your POWER, your LOVE, or both. Maybe something is still in the way of you fully trusting the voice of your SOURCE. Whatever feels even slightly uncomfortable deserves attention and dialogue and will hold valuable opportunities for learning.

Once you feel that your gatherings are flowing with curiosity and ease, you have opened a never-ending flow of support for yourself. Now you are ready to move on to the next exercise.

Exercise XI: Practice. Connection. Anytime. Anywhere.

> *"If we can develop the two sides of ourselves—
> this capacity for love and this capacity for power—
> they will gradually interpenetrate within us."*
> —Robert Johnson

I hope by now that your gatherings with your Inner Support Team have turned into an experience that nourishes you on all levels — body, mind, heart, and soul.

From what my clients tell me, and from my own experience, I can tell you that with continuous practice these gatherings keep getting more and more meaningful.

This brings us to the current exercise. You are continuing to build practices to have meaningful gatherings with your Inner Support Team—in your JournaLogue sessions and beyond.

You may now be beginning to live with an ongoing connection with your Inner Support Team, seeing it for what it always has been, what it is, and what it always will be: a natural, inseparable aspect of you that is always available.

In this exercise, you will explore how to "call" a gathering (connect with the Inner Support Team) and let the members know that you need dialogue with them. You'll learn how to do that anytime, and anywhere.

Your suitable way to consciously connect at any time emerges from your practice. There is no "one size fits all" approach. I have my way, of course, but I don't have words to describe it. For me, it is a state—an energy that I feel and that makes me turn my awareness inward, to issue the internal invitation and to begin my dialogues.

Your practice will enable you to summon your Inner Support Team at any time, day or night, whenever you feel the need. When you convene a gathering outside of your regular JournaLogue sessions, you can still add the dialogue to your journal. Or it can remain an unwritten internal dialogue.

Sometimes you might need the entire team and other times you may only invite individual members into dialogue. Many of us have wonderful mentors in the "outside" world. With the JournaLogue practice, you now also have your group of inner mentors. For me, dialogue with my parts has become such an important habit that I can hardly imagine my life without it.

Before I go into describing the details of the current exercise, let me point something out. From here on, you won't find any suggestions to set your timer for any length of time. In general, my suggestion is to dedicate 35 to 45 minutes for each JournaLogue session, outside of reading the description of the exercises. This has proven to be a useful practice for me, but for you it might be different. If you don't like timing your practice, you might remember the suggestion to hand write three pages or to type 750 words. Those too are suggestions based on practical experience. Please experiment and find out what works best for you.

The Exercise

- Get settled in.

- Before you turn your awareness to your Sacred Space, take time to read everything you have written in Exercise VIII, IX, and X. Try and read slowly, really taking in everything you read.

- Open your journal to a fresh page, and give your page the headline, "Connecting Any Time."

- Begin your gathering as usual.

When you and all your Support Team members are settled in, speak to all of them. Inform them that today you would like to dialogue with each of them around a guiding question you are holding: "how can I practice connecting to you and asking for your support at any given moment?"

You already know your signal(s), you have practices to interrupt your old habitual behaviors, and you know that you now have choices of which you might not have been previously aware. In this gathering, dialogue with every Inner Support Team member. In addition to all this, is there anything you can explore and experiment with? What will support you to connect and communicate with your whole Inner Support Team, or with individual members, at any time?

As always, let it flow. If your parts begin dialoguing with each other about this question, make sure to allow for this. Make space. Listen deeply. Keep journaling.

If you feel that it is time to end the session before you have spoken to each member individually, that's fine. It only means that you need to repeat this exercise until you feel you have all the answers you need.

Take the information you have received and experiment with it in your daily life. Bring your experiences back into the next gathering. Explore and evolve. Maybe it's the same practice you already explored in Exercise VIII. Maybe it's similar, or maybe it's something completely different. Anything that will help you interrupt habitual reactions and turn your awareness to what is needed in a specific moment and is helpful.

Repeat your experimentation until you feel that you have found your own way to turn your awareness inward, connecting to any or all members of your Inner Support Team for help with what is going on for you at any moment.

If you continue practicing this in your everyday life, it will become a habit and an invaluable resource.

The JournaLogue self-coaching practice is grounded on this assumption: when we act from our unified LOVE and POWER we naturally express and manifest our purpose—our soul.

In the course of this program, you have already done a few experiments. I hope that these experiences have given you a taste of what becomes possible when we are aware of our choices.

If you've reached this point in your JournaLogue practice, you are ready to turn directly to your SCENARIO. This is your first experiment of shifting a specific situation or relationship through acting from unified LOVE and POWER, and through that to turn the situation into a manifestation of your unique gift to the world.

Phase 3: Activating Your Resources

Exercise XII: knowing why

> "You are not a drop in the ocean.
> You are the entire ocean in one drop."
> — Rumi

Early in this JournaLogue foundation program you identified your SCENARIO, a situation or relationship that you have repeatedly experienced as unpleasant and that you would like to shift through acting from your unified LOVE and POWER. Since then, you have learned some new practices and done some experiments to prepare yourself, but we have spoken very little about the details of your SCENARIO. It is now time to focus on it.

In this exercise you will explore two questions, together with your Inner Support Team:

- Why is it important for you to shift the experience of this specific situation or relationship?

- "What will your SCENARIO create in your life? What will be new in your life through it?

Before you go into the exercise, please go back in your journal and read what you wrote in Exercise III. Read everything you wrote about your SCENARIO, what it is and, if you could visualize or sense it in any way, how the shifted experience will be when you act from unified LOVE and POWER.

There is always the possibility that since you began with your JournaLogue, this situation or relationship has already shifted because of the exercises and experiments you have gone through. If so, that's awesome! Congratulations! You have already allowed for something wonderful to emerge from the unknown. Make sure to share your experience with your Inner Support Team and, if possible, with other practitioners on lppexperiments.global.

If that is the case, now is the moment to choose another situation or relationship that you would like to shift. Identify a new SCENARIO and to do that, you might consider going through Exercise III again with this new SCENARIO.

After years of practice and after many conversations with clients, I can safely say that we never run out of things that we experience as unpleasant and that we can shift through our own choices.

When you have read through what you wrote in Exercise III or have gone through it again and now have a new SCENARIO, you are ready to step into the current exercise.

The Exercise

- Get situated in your space and ready for your practice.
- After you and your Inner Support Team members have settled into your Sacred Space, open your journal, and write the headline, "Knowing Why."

Then tell your Inner Support Team that in this session you want to explore one question. Write it down: "Why is it important for me to shift the experience of my SCENARIO?"

Keep journaling and write everything that wants to be written. Deeply hold the question and listen very carefully to what comes up. At this point it is unimportant to know where the voices you hear are coming from, or to identify what part is speaking when. Just write everything that comes up while you hold the question.

Here are some things that might come up:

- How the situation has affected you and your life in the past.
- Why you can't simply walk away from it, but rather want to try to improve the experience.

- Your fears, or things that you think might go wrong.
- Your hopes for this shift, and what might become possible.

When nothing more comes up, thank your Inner Support Team for the first round and turn to the second question.

Write in your journal: "What will my SCENARIO create in my life? What will be new in my life through it?"

As before, hold the question, listen deeply, and trust that everything you need to know now about this question will come up. Keep journaling until nothing more comes up. You might even go into dialogue if you have a question about something that arises, or if you feel something is missing. Let it flow until you feel that absolutely everything has emerged, and you have a very strong sense of what will be new for you once you have done your SCENARIO.

As with other exercises, this might take more than one JournaLogue session. That's fine! Once you have a sense that you have gotten everything you need through the answers to these questions, there is one last step to finish this exercise.

Complete the following with one or more sentences in your journal: "Doing my SCENARIO is important because . . ."

If you are not quite sure about what you've written, ask your Inner Support Team for input. Once you feel that what you wrote is complete, that what you have written really feels true to you, then you are ready to move to the next exercise.

Exercise XIII: your wisdom

> "As we fulfill our life's journey and path—
> let us remain trusting
> of the inner guidance of our Soul."
> —Eleesha

Thus far, the exercises of the JournaLogue foundation program have rarely asked you to have a focused dialogue only with your

SOURCE. I am sure your SOURCE has been an important part of your practice. The following exercise will invite you to address some specific questions directly to your SOURCE, and to focus on this dialogue.

Before we continue, let me repeat how we see your SOURCE's role in the JournaLogue.

Your SOURCE holds your deepest wisdom on all levels: mind, body, heart, and spirit. It is always there for you when you need it. It will always help you when you ask it a question. The SOURCE rarely intervenes or speaks without being addressed directly. It often answers back with a question, which in the end gives us a wonderful experience of our own wisdom. So, when you are confused, stuck, unsure of what is going on, don't know who to ask, or need help in any other way, it is best to talk to your SOURCE. When you are experiencing joy and happiness, your SOURCE will love to be in dialogue with you about that as well (as will all other Inner Support Team members).

In preparation for this exercise, please take time to read your entire journal since the beginning of this JournaLogue foundation program. Be aware of your reactions to everything you read, which means paying high attention to your signals while you are reading. Every time you become aware of a signal, take a note. Don't go too deep into it yet, just write down what it is that you read and a few words on why you think that this triggered a signal.

It is important to take short notes of all triggers—those that feel uncomfortable and those that feel nice, or even joyful and heartwarming. Finish this list before you go into the exercise.

The Exercise

- Get yourself and your Inner Support Team all settled in.
- Open your journal and put the headline, "Loving My Signals".

Ask your LOVE, POWER, and SABOTEUR to hold space for this exercise and let them know that in this exercise you will focus on dialogue with your SOURCE.

Turn to your SOURCE and invite it to accompany you closely while you are reading through your list of signals. Ask it to help you see patterns, if there are any. If questions come up as you go through the list, dialogue with your SOURCE about these questions. Write down each question and keep journaling throughout the dialogue. Only stop writing when you go back to reading your list of signals.

Here's an example that Mia from New Zealand shared with me:

"When reading through my list I began to see a pattern that I hadn't been aware of before. I felt a signal every time I read about speaking to people whom I seem to give power over me, purely based on their position (my boss, my sports trainer, and even though I didn't like to admit it, my partner). Then I reached a passage where my POWER had suggested that it would be a great practice for me to turn my attention to my shoulders a few times each day to check if I needed to relax them and drop them down, while at the same time straightening my upper body and raising my head a bit. It suggested that this would help me feel empowered. When I read this in my journal, I realized that I had completely forgotten about it. I wrote this in my list and also wrote that I felt nervous when imagining doing this practice."

"In dialogue with my SOURCE about this, I developed a much better understanding of how my body posture—slightly pulling up my shoulders and lowering my head—was an expression of an issue around disempowering myself. I had been having very useful conversations about this with my SABOTEUR and my POWER. What I hadn't understood was that this specific aspect of my pattern, the embodied expression, needed my attention and that the practice of changing my body posture would support me greatly in stepping into my POWER."

"The discomfort I had felt about this when making my list of signals was about stepping into my POWER, specifically in my intimate relationships. I discovered a belief I was holding that powerful

women aren't sexually attractive. I don't have to tell you what that has done to me and my relationships. When this exercise reminded me of prior dialogues about this, my SOURCE invited me to do nothing else but just remember the suggestion from my POWER—to do the practice with my shoulders, head, and breathing. I have to say: YAY for the small things! I can't tell you how wonderfully this exercise is helping to shift how I experience my relationships, especially with my life partner."

Here are some questions that might be helpful for you in this dialogue about your signals:

- Can you help me better understand where this signal comes from?
- What do you know about it?
- Can you help me shift the experience?

Though this exercise invites you to focus primarily on the dialogue with your SOURCE, other Inner Support Team members might want to contribute as well. Stay attentive to that possibility. If you have a sense that you would like to invite another perspective, turn to your LOVE, POWER, or SABOTEUR, and ask them if there is something they have to say.

You may need a few sessions to finish this exercise, but once you are complete with the dialogue about your signal list there is one more step to do before you can move on. Ask each of your Inner Support Team members this question: "How does what I have learned from this exercise apply to my SCENARIO?"

This last step alone might take up a whole session or several. This is just fine. As you go through with this step, however long it takes, I am sure it will be an additional source of valuable perspectives and learnings. Once you have collected all these inputs, you are ready to move on to the next exercise.

Before we move on though, let's check in with your awareness of your signals. We won't directly address them further in the remainder of this JournaLogue program, but please keep practicing with your signals. Doing that is like building a muscle and it will prepare you for situations including and beyond your SCENARIO. This strengthened capacity will stay with you in the future, helping you shift any situation that you initially experienced as disturbing or unpleasant into an experience that you can accept as an opportunity to learn from—if you decide that is what you want at that moment. You always have the choice.

When I first began to practice with my signals, I was shocked to find out how often during the course of a day I was triggered, and in how many ways. After a while I found that most of my triggers came from a pattern of judgment, which wasn't a particularly comfortable realization. Until then I had believed myself to be pretty non-judgmental.

I realized I had held an expectation that the practice of shifting my experiences through connecting to my LOVE and POWER and acting from the awareness of unifying these resources would reduce the number of triggers for me. Writing this today makes me smile, because eventually I realized that this expectation was clearly grounded in a desire to become a "better person". My old "when/then" pattern was showing up again. For me, this stood for being disconnected from self-love.

Sometimes, this journey felt too complex. Sometimes I got sucked into a spiral of doubt and frustration. Through my dialogues with my Inner Support Team, I eventually learned to accept that there is simply always more to learn. I have good and not so good days, and all this is part of my unique journey. Most days, I can see the gift of it all. These practices are not about "fixing myself" or "resolving" something, but about being with what's true for me, about remaining curious, joyful, and at ease to the greatest extent possible in any given moment, and about exploring what is mine to do next.

Just to make sure there is no misunderstanding here, being curious, joyful, and at ease doesn't mean ignoring my and others' pain, grief, or trauma. It means surrendering to what are inevitable parts of life. We can experience what flows through us, let it teach us, and at some point, make the choice to let it go . . . moving on, and continuing our journey with curiosity about what is up for us next.

> "Nothing ever goes away until it has taught us what we need to know."
>
> —Pema Chödrön[33]

The invitation to you is to keep noticing your signals, no matter how small, and to experiment with how you can best shift the experience of the situation through connecting to your LOVE and POWER as a response to your signals.

Exercise XIV: your core psychological needs

> "Don't be afraid of your fears. They're not there to scare you. They are there to let you know that something is worth it."
>
> —C. JoyBell C.

I love this quote. It always makes me feel humble and grateful for the great miracle of life.

As part of this miracle, isn't it amazing how much wisdom we carry inside ourselves? Everything you've discovered since the beginning of this JournaLogue program has come from within—these aren't lessons that someone else needs to teach you. You can trust that everything is right there, available to you at all times, ready to be explored and integrated.

Trust. What a magical word.

When something is up for us and we need input and support, we have a place to go: our Sacred Space, with its amazing resources . . . our Inner Support Team.

---

[33] https://pemachodronfoundation.org/

The current exercise has two parts. They invite you to communicate with these amazing resources, to explore something important: the fear of not getting your core needs met. This fear always plays a role when changing something in your life.

Any time we reflect on and sense into what is up next for us, we are guided by a number of underlying needs. These either energize us or get in the way of our motivation to move forward.

Our fears can get in the way. These fears are important and hold vital information. Trying to ignore them will lead us to move forward without learning something essential about ourselves—something we will eventually need. When ignored or pushed aside, the fears find ways to reappear and get in our way. This pattern will continue until we either give up on our growth and movement or turn towards the fears and integrate them.

Different traditions and schools of thought offer different definitions of our core psychological needs. In general, they fall under these categories:

- The need to be loved and be accepted for who we are—to have a sense of belonging.

- The need for autonomy, freedom, and independence—to be in control of our own life.

- The need to feel safe, to avoid pain, and to express oneself authentically—to experience life as good.

- The need to grow, to enhance self-esteem, and to feel competent—to progress in life.

When we feel that our choices, actions, and experiences align with or increase the fulfillment of our core needs, we feel motivated to move forward. When we perceive a change as a threat to one of our core needs, even subconsciously, we experience fear. Understandably, this decreases motivation and holds us back from moving forward. We are often unaware of when and how these underlying needs influence our decisions and behaviors.

The Exercise (Part 1)

To begin, take a moment to connect to your SCENARIO. Visualize the new way in which you will experience this situation and/or relationship. Imagine the place, the people, and the context. See yourself going through this experience or interaction as you are acting from your unified LOVE and POWER.

When you feel connected to your SCENARIO, read the following statements slowly, and at least twice. Pay very close attention to your inner reactions when reading. These are signals! While each of these statements might be true for you in its own way, we each have a general tendency to hold one as more important than the others. The objective is to find out which of the statements resonates most with you.

Take a deep breath. Now read.

1. When going through with my SCENARIO I want to make sure to remain loved and accepted for who I am.

2. When going through with my SCENARIO I want to make sure to remain autonomous and independent.

3. When going through with my SCENARIO I want to make sure to remain safe.

4. When going through with my SCENARIO I want to make sure to feel good about myself.

When you have read each statement at least twice, decide for yourself—which of these sentences feels most true? Which one is most important to you?

- Once you have a sense of which is the most important core need for you, begin a JournaLogue session in your Sacred Space, with your Inner Support Team.

- Write the headline, "My Core Needs, Part 1" and immediately begin to journal.

First, tell your Inner Support Team members about your experience when reading the statements. Share with them your sense of which of the core needs is most important for you. Tell them about the signals you sensed, and if you identified any of those signals as fears. Reflect on the signals and fears.

Once you have told your story, ask your Inner Support Team members for input. Ask them to help you to see everything there is for you to learn in this exercise. Listen very carefully to their input, and make sure to ask any questions that might come up for you.

Continue the conversation until the end of the time you've given yourself for this session. Continue with this exercise for as many sessions as you need. Make sure you explore everything that feels even the slightest bit like a fear. Trust your signals—it will be worth it!

When you feel that you have covered everything in this part of the exercise, you can move on to the second part.

In part 1 we experienced how important it is to ensure that our core needs are met, especially when we intend to change something in our life. To ensure our core needs are met, we tend to follow specific behavior patterns that unconsciously guide us. In many cases these patterns get in the way of expressing who we truly are.

Can you remember a situation where you were confronted with the necessity to make a decision and you felt fearful, or maybe even threatened, when considering the possible consequences? Perhaps your job changed, and you weren't sure if you would be able to do the new job as well as the old one. Maybe you were offered a promotion or wanted to look for a new position. Maybe you and your partner had a disagreement about a holiday destination, or about which new car to buy. Maybe you learned that the lease on your home wouldn't be renewed, and though you had come to love your home you knew you were faced with a move.

Please take a moment to think about a situation where you had to make a decision but were either afraid of what might happen or didn't feel you had a choice. In such a scenario, we tend to react in one of several common ways:

- We take assertive, clear action, requesting or demanding what we think we need. We speak up, or even raise our voice, in order to avoid options that feel like a threat to our core needs.

- We don't speak up, but we increase our activity and work harder to show that we "deserve" the solution that will meet our core needs.

- We withdraw ourselves and our attention from the threatening situation, avoid our thoughts, our feelings, and even the people involved. We passively hope that things will unfold in a way that meets our core needs.

Do you recognize yourself in these descriptions? The behaviors are neither bad nor good. They are simply patterns, and the thing about patterns is that we tend to use them on autopilot. This costs us the chance to make a choice with clear awareness of what is needed now, in this particular moment.

The Exercise (Part 2)

Part 1 and Part 2 of this exercise are closely connected but should be done during separate journaling sessions. Other practices might invite you to work with just your SABOTEUR, but in the JournaLogue process we have a whole Inner Support Team to work with. This team includes the befriended SABOTEUR. Its perspective on all this is very important—as are the perspectives of each team member.

Here are the steps for Part 2 of this exercise:

- Open your journal and write the headline, "My Core Needs, Part 2".

- Gather with your Support Team in your Sacred Space, as usual.

First, turn to you SABOTEUR. Invite it to a conversation about your fears and your typical behaviors when fear comes up. Do you tend to be assertive, speaking up about your needs? Do you tend to work harder to "earn" what you feel you need? Or do you tend to pull back and avoid everything having to do with the threat, hoping that this will lead to your needs getting met, one way or the other?

Remember, your SABOTEUR is your "Guardian of Choice". In relationship with this light side of your SABOTEUR, you can now explore your choices.

You can begin your dialogue with questions like:

- How will I recognize when my behavior is guided by an unconscious pattern?
- How can you support me to shift at this moment? To make my decisions based on conscious choices, rooted in awareness of the present moment?

It is important that you invite your full Inner Support Team into the conversation as well, to explore how each member can help support you.

Let the dialogue flow. Listen, let the members talk to each other, ask questions, be with what wants to emerge, and keep writing until the time is over.

If you have a sense that there is more to explore, as always, do as many JournaLogue sessions with this exercise as you need.

Once you feel you have explored everything that is currently available to know about your fears and how to deal with them, there is one last step to this exercise: read through everything you journaled during parts 1 and 2 of this exercise and make a list of your learnings.

Write the headline, "while going through with my SCENARIO I can make sure to get my core needs met by doing the following:"

You can check back with your Inner Support Team members if questions come up while collecting your learnings, or to see if you have forgotten something important.

When you read the list and feel that it gives you motivation and comfort in moving forward, then you are done with this part of the JournaLogue journey.

Exercise XV: favorable conditions

> "In the presence of your own loving attention, you create the inner conditions that are necessary to step into the next greatest evolution of yourself."
> —Debbie Ford

With this exercise you will start to shift the focus of your JournaLogue sessions to your LOVE and POWER. It is important that you still do your Welcome Ritual and connect to all Inner Support Team members at the beginning. Next time you enter your Sacred Space for a dialogue, inform your SOURCE and your SABOTEUR that, for the time being, you will focus on your dialogues with LOVE and POWER. Tell SOURCE and SABOTEUR that you would like them to hold space for these dialogues.

Of course, your SOURCE and SABOTEUR might still want to contribute. If that is the case, make sure to listen to these inputs as well. In general, SOURCE and SABOTEUR are happy to hold space for your more focused dialogues with LOVE and POWER.

Before you go into the next meeting with your Inner Support Team, go back and read everything you wrote in Exercise VIII (YAY for the Small Things). In that exercise, you identified a practice with LOVE and POWER that would help you to shift from reacting to any one of your signals in a habitual way (on autopilot) to making a choice—deciding to act, as far as possible in any given moment, from unified LOVE and POWER.

Once you have read through everything you journaled in Exercise VIII you can begin the current exercise.

The Exercise

Can you remember the beginning of your JournaLogue journey? You began with creating supportive outer and inner conditions for your journaling sessions. In this exercise, you will do something similar. To the greatest extent possible, given where you are today, you will prepare to create supportive outer and inner conditions for your SCENARIO.

Begin your gathering in your Sacred Space as usual, writing "Favorable Conditions" as the headline in your journal.

Begin this gathering with a question:

"How can I best create supportive outer and inner conditions for my SCENARIO?"

"Outer conditions" are things like scheduling, location, context (sharing a meal, taking a walk, sitting down in a formal meeting), or maybe other concrete steps to get ready—perhaps preparing documents, or bringing a little gift.

"Inner conditions" are for you to feel good physically, mentally, and emotionally. This can include getting enough sleep, eating well and staying hydrated, meditating, exercising, playing a sport, taking a walk, recharging in nature, or whatever else supports you.

While journaling about your preparations, it is important to notice any signals, or subtle physical and emotional sensations triggering various forms of discomfort. You have honed your awareness of those signals and practiced how to deal with them. You already know that they point toward something you need to look out for. They invite you to explore why they are there and what can be learned from them.

You can be sure that if you are not fully comfortable with what you intend to do, something will likely get in your way. If you get a signal while journaling, make sure to address it. To find out what it is about, you might ask for input from your LOVE and POWER. Perhaps you'll also ask for perspectives from your SOURCE and SABOTEUR. Capture everything you learn.

Whether it takes one or multiple gatherings, you'll arrive at a sense that you are well prepared. When this happens, take time to read everything you have written in this exercise. Underline or otherwise mark the necessary preparations to create the best supportive outer and inner conditions for your SCENARIO.

To the greatest extent possible, you have made sure that you are ready to turn towards embodying your SCENARIO.

You are ready to step into the unknown, to experiment with how your experience of this specific situation and/or relationship will shift when you act from unified LOVE and POWER in service to your purpose—the unique gift that is yours to contribute.

Phase 4: Your SCENARIO

An ongoing experiment with the unknown

> "What lies behind us and what lies ahead of us
> are tiny matters compared to what lies within us."
> —Henry David Thoreau

When you are ready to begin your SCENARIO, you have reached the end of the JournaLogue foundation program. The exercises of Phase 4 have no numbers and no titles. How to approach them is totally up to you.

The invitation is to begin to embody your SCENARIO and continue your gatherings in your Sacred Space with your Inner Support Team.

Your Inner Support Team will support you and will remain available for you through your experiments with your SCENARIO, and beyond. This team will be there for you whenever you need support in acting from unified LOVE and POWER. They can help you trust yourself to experiment with many situations that arise in life, and through doing so to gift yourself with new experiences and new possibilities.

We never know where our intentions and decisions will take us, yet we always have the choice to experiment, learn, fail, succeed, learn some more, remain curious, and step further into the unknown.

Your Inner Support Team has always been there and will always be there for you. You will decide how often you want to explicitly access your inner resources through the methods described in this program. I hope you will take what you've learned and continue with the practice.

It is really important for you to know that you are not alone on this journey!

7

Your Gifts Meet the World's Needs

If it weren't for the JournaLogue practice and my Inner Support Team, I believe I wouldn't have been able to make my personal purpose so central to my life. It enabled me to say "yes", where I formerly probably would have said "no", and vice versa. Without this, I wouldn't have found the courage to speak my voice around the unification of love and power in service to purpose. I would have missed making connections to so many beautiful people and communities all over the world. I would have missed the opportunity to adopt a nomadic lifestyle and expand the places for me to manifest my work in the world. Ultimately, without this practice, I would never have written this book.

I am in continuous dialogue with my Inner Support Team. It is an ongoing journey of experimenting with how to manifest the unification of love and power. I try, I learn, I fail, I succeed, I laugh, I cry, I share with others who are on their own experimental journeys. I am touched and inspired by their stories and deeply grateful for what I can learn from them.

Like Alice, who joined a "Love, Power, and Purpose" program in January 2020 knowing she wanted to help make the world a more peaceful and healthier place . . . but not knowing how. Alice left that weekend feeling profoundly drawn to touching the lives of children beyond her own. The clarity Alice arrived at during the program helped her say "yes" when a vacancy needed to be filled on her local public school board, and she stepped up to apply. Now, she's serving as an elected school board member and working with others at the local and state level to help public education better serve the social, emotional, and academic needs of all students.

Or John, who told me that he finally decided to apply to speak at a conference about what had been at the core of his personal journey for years. He had never, until now, had the courage to show himself in all his authenticity—and he was accepted as a keynote speaker.

Or Maria, who shifted her approach to how she relates with others when in conflict. This completely redefined her relationship with her husband, her daughter, and her mother—and, after not too long, led her into a different professional career. She joined a nonprofit to engage in the climate emergency, working on an issue she deeply cared for but had previously found unbearable to step into as it always led her into conversations loaded with conflict. Today she can have difficult conversations while remaining both loving and powerful.

As I am coming to the end of writing this book, my biggest current experiment is around an old pattern that is showing up again: I tend to overload myself with too many commitments, with the result that I lose focus of what is important in any given moment. It reduces my presence and consequently the love I have for what I am doing, and it makes me feel less powerful. I know that my Inner Support Team will help me through it. I know what I am called to do: to trust and to stay aware, to take responsibility for the node that I am in the web of life, and to remain open and curious about the next learning step that life is offering.

There is always something to explore and to learn and it is always a new story. We all have fascinating stories to tell. They are beautifully unique, yet at the same time completely connected. Like everything and everyone, we are each here for a reason. We all bring unique gifts to the world.

How many places in the world are calling for someone with the gifts *you* have to give, from a place of unified love and power? What kind of experiment do you want to be a part of? What's the right fit of *your* talents with the world's great needs?

I invite you to come join me and other JournaLogue practitioners and purpose agents on lppexperiments.global. Help build and grow a global community that collectively explores the question, "what becomes possible when we act from unified love and power in service of the greater whole?"

Bring your gifts to others through sharing the stories of your experiments. Through acting from unified love and power, what has shifted or become possible for you? No story is too small or too big. The more stories we share, the more others will be inspired to join and to begin their own experiments with the unknown and experience how acting from unified love and power can change their lives and the lives of their families and friends. Beyond, the ripples continue—these shifts can impact communities, companies, institutions, societies, and who knows what else!

We as a species are facing many existential questions, and no single person can know the answers. If we—individually and collectively—can allow the liberation of not knowing to unfold, we will be able to lovingly and powerfully experiment with the unknown. Let's learn, fail forward, and continue to experiment together . . . and maybe, through one small step after the other, uncover the *Web of Unified Love AS and Power As* that is there, always, and indefinitely.

Through the JournaLogue practice, you can experience a method for growing your capacity to individually act from unified love and power in service to purpose. Here's what you, and I, and all others that will join us, can explore together: what becomes possible when we expand this capacity to the human collective?

Calling out to you

Let me repeat the question at the core of this book: what becomes possible when we act from unified love and power in service of the more-than-human world? Perhaps this is easier to approach in a more granular fashion. Let's break it down:

By acting from unified love and power in service of the more-than-human world:

- How can our relationships to one another, and to spirit-consciousness-nature, shift?

- How can the consequences of colonization—supremacy, racism, inequity, and injustice in all its forms—shift?

- How can the way we deal with the climate emergency shift?

- How can parenting shift?

- How can education and entire educational systems shift?

- How can work, organizing, and the entire field of business shift?

- How can medical care and entire medical systems shift?

- How can political and judicial systems shift?

- How can economies shift?

So many more questions are possible . . . what possibilities can you dream of?

From where I am standing, there is not a single issue or system that can't benefit from asking this same question.

The important thing is, *we don't know*! We don't know what changes are coming, but hopefully through our JournaLogue journey we *do* know that surprising transformation becomes possible when we move from habituated actors running on autopilot to being aware, well-resourced, choiceful people acting from unified love and power in service to purpose.

If you feel a signal—an emotional reaction, no matter how small or large—while reading the questions listed above, or if you have one or more questions to add, let me call out to you: you have a unique contribution to make, and you are not alone. Begin your experiment now and tell your story.

From now forward

This is my entreaty: begin your own individual experiments. Join the community at lppexperiments.global and allow me to host you. Find others who feel drawn to similar questions. Together, begin collective experiments. Step into the unknown, explore what wants to emerge, experiment, learn, fail forward, continue to experiment. You will make a difference. You might even set something life-altering in motion.

This book is only the beginning, and it is not for me to finish. As I've already discovered—I DON'T KNOW. In the not knowing there lies possibility!

We need community. We need collective emergence. We need each other to lovingly and powerfully write this book on. Please share your stories, your individual and collective experiments, and the changes they are creating. Let's write on, together.

May this work never be finished!

Acknowledgements

Writing a book is a challenging and incredibly rewarding journey. It is almost impossible to describe the support I received that made this book possible, and the tremendous gratitude I feel. I will try to do it justice in some small way.

Let me begin with the most important person in my life: my son Conrad. Ever since the moment you entered my life, you have been a boundless source of unconditional love, appreciation, laughs and tears, inspiration and learning, and so much more. Thank you for giving me the gift of motherhood and the life-enriching experiences it never ceases to offer.

My sister Gabriele is always there for me. She knows that I need an emotional home even more than a physical one, and she provides this for me with the most beautiful sisterly love anyone could wish for. Without you, Sis, I wouldn't have made it. Thank you–I love you to bits.

I am forever grateful to my very special friend and colleague Tom Thomison. Working together and experiencing the growth of our friendship over more than a decade have given me many of the most important insights that inspired this book. Your way of always showing up as who you truly are, and of inviting me to do the same, and your way of being available for and interested in this version of us in this very moment, form a foundation for the unique and deep friendship we have. Tom, I am immeasurably grateful for our loving friendship and for your many ways of showing your support.

This book would not have been written without the ongoing support of my dear friend and editor Marnie Jackson. The way you sense into what I have written (with English not being my mother tongue), ask the right questions, listen carefully to what I intend to express and then work your magic with words, is amazing. Your capacity for this work brings my stories to life. I really don't have the words to thank you enough for being my midwife in this birthing process.

Let me now turn to my most meaningful professional contexts, encode.org and Evolution at Work—two self-organized enterprises I was fortunate enough to co-found. My gratitude goes out to every single one of you, who engaged in those two enterprises together with me, for no matter how long. Each of you has contributed to my learning in a very special way. Thank you from the bottom of my heart for being part of my journey: (in alphabetical order) Robert Anaars, Jo Aschenbrenner, Mihai Banulescu, Gary Baron, Jennifer Benson, Linda Berens, Ranjit Bhagwandas, Britta Bibel-Cavallaro, Andrew Brown, Joel DeJong, Stefan Faatz-Ferstl, Rashid Gilanpour, Floris Hammer, Floris Huetnik, Peter Kessels, Monika Kletzmayr, Ivana Kljakovic-Gaspic, Anke Lessmann, David P. Lima, Erik Lundquist, Jonathan Misrahi, Sylvain Montreuil, Nick Osborne, Richard Pircher, Björn Rabethge, Lori Rock, Lermit Rosell, Katharina Schwarz, Simon Schwarz, Nathan Snyder, Tom Thomison, Will VanInvagen, Melinda Varfi, João Wackernagel, and Dennis Witrock.

When I realized that I needed financial support to be able to focus fully on writing, I decided to launch a crowdfunding campaign. Help arrived, from so many, in a shower of love and support. This gift of being helped is something I will hold onto for the rest of my life. I couldn't have done it without your support: Gary Baron, Angelica Blass, Marcus Druen, Ikuo Eno, Alex Eunkyeong

Yu, Mónica Expositor Blasco, Stefan Faatz-Ferstl, Andrea Fare, Stefanie Gfeller, Simone Groß, Alexandra Guild, Hiroaki Hasegawa, Marius Hogendoorn, Georg Holzknecht, Hanna Hündorf, Jennifer Hurshell, Hypoport SE/Björn Schneider, Mie Iinuma, Hiroaki Ishii, Cyrille Jegu, Kenshu Kamura, Monika Kletzmayr, Ivana Kljakovic-Gaspic, Kanae Kuwahara, Anke Lessmann, Erik Lundquist, Brooke McNamara, Ryo Nakadoi, Iurii Nikolenko, Noriko Ogami, Ines Ornig, Sanjay Rajan, Lori Rock, Rika Sagishima, Max Semenchuk, Olga Solokchik, Thomas Thomison, Nikki Thompson, Leslie van Berkum, Karina van Berkum, João Wackernagel, Gabriele Wanderer, Dennis Wittrock, Kenichi Yasuda.

I wouldn't have had the courage to publish this book without the invaluable feedback from my first readers. Ruth Gerhard, Hanna Hühndorf, Doug Kirkpatrick, Anke Lessmann, Autumn Preble, Tom Thomison, and Nikki Thompson–the book was greatly improved, and I was greatly encouraged, by your feedback. Thank you so much for engaging in this way, investing your time and expertise to give me yet another level of support in this project.

Expressing my gratitude within my professional contexts would be incomplete without naming Holacracy. For more than a decade this practice has been a challenger and a teacher. It set me off on a learning journey I never expected and I gratefully acknowledge that to this day, it is a practice that keeps challenging me, that triggers my curiosity, and that invites me to continuously learn more.

I deeply hope that within this book's pages I have sufficiently expressed my gratitude to the many other methods and wonderful teachers without whose inspiring wisdom I would not be where I am today.

Last, but not least, I would like to speak to a very unique place and its people who welcomed and enchanted me: the small Greek island of Halki, island of friendship and peace. Both the island and the community opened my heart and soul with their welcoming embrace, supporting me to begin the process of writing this book.

The land and community of Halki, it turned out, also kept me returning to finish my writing. My heart is forever connected in gratitude to Halki and my friends there who so lovingly and joyfully held space for the emergence of *New Stories of Love, Power, and Purpose*.

About the Author

Christiane is a seasoned entrepreneur, an international business consultant, coach, and speaker, and a global pioneer in the field of self-organization and purpose-guided work.

She has spent the past decade striving to better understand the shift in power systems triggered by self-organization and its effect on the people concerned.

Christiane sought an approach that would address the disconnection and disruption she witnessed in herself and others, and through this work discovered exciting new stories of love and power and their implications for people and planet.

Following the call of her own personal purpose—"The unification of love and power"—led Christiane to let go of old stories and to embrace the liberation of what is emerging in their place—an experience that led eventually to this book.

Christiane was born in Austria and has a son, Conrad. Today, she considers herself to be a citizen of the world and has adopted a nomadic lifestyle, sharing time between several of her favorite communities and places around the globe.

Made in United States
Troutdale, OR
10/02/2023

13345699R00152